THE
SHADOW

The interest in the Christocentric nature of the Scripture is not only an academic discussion. The person in the pew wants to know if there is a real storyline to the assembled Scriptures. What a thrill to find that the storyline is the exaltation of Christ through the redemption of man! With thoughtful prose and a warm style, Ryan Dalgliesh makes this truth real for the reader. I encourage you to let Ryan help you see God's plan unfolding in the Scriptures!

—Dr. Steven Smith
Associate Dean for Professional Doctorates
Southwestern Baptist Theological Seminary
Fort Worth, TX

The Shadow is a passionate plea for people to behold Christ. It is drenched in truth and saturated with rhetoric. This collision of Old Testament scripture and stimulating poetry fueled in me a deeper affection for Jesus. May the revelation of God through this study renew your sense of awe and wonder of our unsearchable God, and move your heart to respond in worship.

—Matt Boswell
Worship Pastor
Fellowship of the Parks (PGA hopeful)

In *The Shadow* Old Testament stories burst to life. It is filled with fresh insights into the power and the purpose of God. I sensed the fear and felt the pain and the joy of the human struggle of deliverance. I was encouraged as I saw how the silhouette of the Savior is clearly cast across all the pages of scripture.

—John Strappazon
Collegiate Ministries Specialist

THE
SHADOW

ryan dalgliesh

TATE PUBLISHING & Enterprises

Published by Tate Publishing & Enterprises, LLC
127 E. Trade Center Terrace | Mustang, Oklahoma 73064 USA
1.888.361.9473 | www.tatepublishing.com

Tate Publishing is committed to excellence in the publishing industry. The company reflects the philosophy established by the founders, based on Psalm 68:11,
"The LORD *gave the word and great was the company of those who published it."*

Book design copyright © 2010 by Tate Publishing, LLC. All rights reserved.
Cover artowrk by Christy Honea
Cover design by Amber Gulilat
Interior design by Jeff Fisher

Published in the United States of America

ISBN: 978-1-61566-642-3
1. Religion, Christian Theology, Soteriology
2. Religion, Biblical Studies, Old Testament
10.04.14

DEDICATION

I want to dedicate this book to my son Asher Ethan Dalgliesh. It is my deep prayer and longing that you would grow into a man who is passionately in love with the Jesus who died to save mankind, and that you would love the Word of God by which we live.

I love you.

THANKS

There are a ton of people who gave me input on these chapters or helped me in some way during the writing of this book, so I would like to take the time to thank them. Thanks so much Kevin Kirkland. Turnabout is fair play. I looked over your great book. Thanks for looking over mine. Kristin Booth, I am amazed that you took the time to critique each chapter with the overwhelming amount of work you had in seminary. Thanks. Elizabeth McMillen, my sweet cousin, thanks for great input and for reading this while you sought to manage your three kiddos. BJ Stewart, we'll always have our first camp. That was great. Thanks for your encouragement with every chapter. Christy Honea, you do great design work. Thanks. I also want to thank Jason Holt, Gene Ferrell, Bryan Waddell, Mom, Dad, Carolyn Curtis, Ryan and Sarah Bebee, Kelsey Carter, Josh Edinger and Mugshot Coffee House, Frankie Levings, Lakan Mariano, Micah Mariano, Jason Williams, Dan Bailey, and Steve Hemphill. All the conversations we had and ideas I bounced off of you helped me so much.

Thanks to Dr. Steven Smith at SWBTS in Fort Worth for being so gracious as to review this book for me. Thanks to my college pastor John Strappazon, who taught me so much about discipleship and loving the Word, for reviewing this project. It is fun to share it with you.

Thanks to the pastors who continue to preach the Word of God and whose ministries continue to impact my own; Colin Smith, Pastor of The Orchard Evangelical Free Church in Arlington Heights; John Piper, Pastor of Bethlehem Baptist Church in Minneapolis; and Ravi Zacharias, speaker and apologist of Ravi Zacharias International Ministries.

I also want to thank my wife, Michele, for constantly encouraging me on this project. You are daily a blessing to me. Thanks for reading it for me. Thanks for loving me. Thanks for helping me to love Jesus more. You are my prize!

Most importantly I have to thank my God and Father who, though I was a sinner, set his love upon me. He put into place a beautiful plan of redemption and salvation from the beginning of all time that would be fulfilled in his Son, Jesus the Christ. He wove together a beautiful tapestry in the Scriptures explaining to us over and over again the salvation that is found in Jesus alone.

Thank you, Jesus, for dying to redeem fallen, sinful man.

Thank you, Holy Spirit, for helping us to understand the Bible as it reveals Jesus to us.

TABLE OF CONTENTS

FOREWORD

Never before in human history has there been a time when the truths of God's infallible Word were more important than right now. With the immense skepticism of the church in today's America and the complete disregard for the absolutes of the Bible, we find ourselves with very few choices about the future. The only choice we can make that will ensure our children can live out the call of the God of the Bible is to once again make the Word of God the centerpiece of all things. I have known Ryan Dalgliesh for over five years, and our friendship has been life changing for me. Ryan is on a mission to bring the Bible back to the forefront of our churches, our homes, and our lives. His passion for the truths of the Bible are contagious, and his deep understanding of the Scriptures is founded on years of study, prayer, and revelation only given by the Holy Spirit himself. If there is one thing I have learned from my friend Ryan, it is that the Bible is a complete work from beginning to end detailing the redemptive love of God founded in the sacrifice of his son Jesus for all mankind. The Bible, from beginning to end is about Jesus.

The book you are about to read is an incredible masterpiece of imagery, theology, and the overwhelming truth of God's eternal plan to rescue us from our sin through his son Jesus. Ryan reveals to us the gospel found not only in Matthew, Mark, Luke, and John but long before those men even existed. You are about to meet Jesus in the Garden of Eden, the ladder of Jacob, the hidden manna of Moses, in the lion's den of Daniel, and in the sweet tree that transformed the bitter water of Marah. *The Shadow* has caused me to run to the Word of God in search of Jesus in every book of the Bible, and I have found him there over and over—crucified, risen, and coming again to take his bride the church unto himself. I cannot wait for you to read it. I cannot wait to read it to my children and explain to them that Noah's Ark was not just a big boat; it was a shadow of the Savior that was to come—he is Jesus. Whether you are a scholar, a pastor, a parent, or even a skeptic, the revelations found in this book, are going to change the way you see the Bible and the Savior found in its pages. You will gain a deep understanding of God's plan to save us by grace not according to our own efforts, the purpose of his wrath, and the overwhelming nature of his unfailing love. I pray that as you meet Jesus in each chapter, the LORD captures your soul and draws you back to the Bible, and that you commit your life to sharing the story of Jesus with a lost and dying world.

Thank you Ryan for your incredible friendship, your love and support, but most of all, thank you for inspiring me to fall deeply in love with the Word that made its dwelling among us—with our eternal Savior, Jesus.

—Kevin D. Kirkland
Founder of Katalyst Ministries
Author of *Broken Walls: And Those Called to Repair Them*

INTRODUCTION

I am about to be a father. In fact by the time you find yourself reading these words I will have been a daddy to my little boy for quite a while. When I found out September 21, 2008 that my wife was pregnant I was so excited. She woke me up that Sunday morning just hours before I was supposed to preach at my friend's church in San Antonio and shoved the pregnancy test in front of my blurry eyes. I couldn't believe it! The very first thing I did was take hold of Michele and pray, "God, I thank you so much for this child that you have given to us. I pray that this child would come to know you at an early age and would honor, love, and glorify you with its entire life." That has continued to be my prayer for my son and will be until the day I die.

But the truth is, I find as I have endeavored to write these pages with you in mind, that my heart has been stirred up for you. I want you to know Jesus. I don't want you to just have some cognitive assent to his person, I want you to really know him. I want you to be passionately and deeply in love with the great and beautiful Savior. I'm not sure if you have been in church for many years or if Jesus is a distant and foreign concept to you. I don't know if you are bitter towards all things God related or if you find yourself wounded and searching for hope. However, I am certain that the answer for everything related to life is found in none but Jesus.

When we read the Bible we must conclude that Jesus is at the center of everything. One of my favorite verses for some years now is found in Colossians and says, "Therefore no one is to act as your judge in regard to food or drink or in respect to a festival or a new moon or a Sabbath day—things which are a mere shadow of what is to come; but the substance belongs to Christ" (2:16–17). These verses are amazing as they show us that the things of the Old Testament law are shadow only and have no substance in themselves. The entire Old Testament is summed up in Christ alone. If you do not have an understanding of the Bible that has Jesus as the focal point, as the very linchpin of the whole history of mankind, then you have settled for a "mere shadow." Hopefully, my efforts here will reveal the centrality of Christ in all things historical and eternal as they pertain to the Bible and to life itself.

The message of salvation has been painted for you on every page of the Scriptures. You may find it difficult at times to see it. You may find yourself discouraged because you don't seem to understand, but let me assure you that you can know the truth of Jesus in the Bible in an intimate fashion. Luke records for us in his first book, "…and beginning with Moses and all the

Prophets, Jesus explained to them what was said in all the Scriptures concerning himself" (Luke 24:27).

I haven't undertaken the overwhelming task of explaining all of the Scripture to you, but I hope that this will draw you in.

One day not very far from now, I plan on taking my little boy and cradling him in my arms from the first breath he takes and speaking the name Jesus over his life. There is no other name given among men on earth by which we *must* be saved.

The story of Jesus has been told millions of times, and it never ceases to move in power. Lives are changed, families restored, sinners rescued, and souls are redeemed! Perhaps you know the Name and have come to love it, or perhaps you find yourself skeptical as I say these words. Either way, journey through these pages with me. Skip around if you want to. Walk through the story of the Bible with me and see how many different ways the person and power of Jesus have been painted for us to take in. Admittedly I have taken some poetic license to fill in parts of the story we do not know, but at the end of each chapter I have included all of the Scripture that was used so that you can see I have not strayed from teaching the truth of the text. While many of these Old Testament stories are shadows and forerunners of the Savior, Jesus, keep in mind that we can't follow every example to its logical conclusion. We will seek to take the stories only as far as the Scripture itself does.

I have made these chapters, and this book as a whole, short for a reason.

I want you to pick it up.

I want you to read it.

I want you to recommend it to friends. I've been a Christian for thirty years and yet I find myself sometimes forgetting how beautiful the story of Jesus and the salvation he brings truly is.

Soon Asher (my little boy) will be in my arms, and I will start this way: "Once upon a time God loved you so much that he sent Jesus…" There in the stillness of his nursery by the gentle glow of a nightlight I will begin in Genesis and unfold the beautiful story of salvation. He won't understand me at first. He'll whimper a bit as I rock him to sleep. I'll give him a little kiss on the top of his head and lay him in his bed, and as I turn to walk out the door, I'll whisper: "Tomorrow I'll tell you about Jesus in the book of Exodus."

I don't know where you are right now, maybe on your couch or in an airport waiting for your flight. Maybe you are in your bed just getting ready to call it a day. Perhaps you have found yourself at a coffee shop just trying to squeeze in a few pages before you have to return to work. Wherever you are, I want to say, "Let me tell you a story. I won't take much of your time. But I must tell you the most wonderful news in the entire world."

And as you work your way through these pages, my desire is that you would know of the tremendous love that God has for you that he would make a way for you to be saved. My prayer is that as that knowledge finds a place in your heart that you would find yourself more in love with Jesus and the Bible, which speaks of him more than you ever have before. If you have questions about how to be saved, please contact me through my website on the back of the book.

Do you have a few minutes?

Are you comfortable?

Do you need anything?

Then let me begin, "Once upon a time, God loved you so much that he sent Jesus…"

GENESIS 1:

"In the beginning... "

"In the beginning God created the heavens and the earth" (1). So begins the story of life! In that moment when God, who had been from antiquity eternally existing, first set light and darkness on the stage of time and dotted space with galaxies spiraling with their many planets, Christ was there! In that deep sigh when formless worlds took shape and earth was colored blue with seas and lands were drawn together in grand design, and green ran across the ground in creeping vines and sprung from the dark soil in towering trees, Christ was working! When first the light was justified by a burning sun pulsing with energy and the moon hung forever in its circle as a mirror of his brother's glory, and when shape was first given to the dark blanket as every pinprick of light pierced the black canvas of night through many myriad stars, Christ was the maker! In that heartbeat of a moment when silent deeps first teemed with life and great fishes were first schooling and darting through bright and brilliant corals, and when birds first felt the great wind beneath their fragile bones and now both the lows and the highs of creation were sought out, it was Christ that put them there! When the final touches of a brushstroke painted herds of beasts in great yellow fields, and mighty forms were first placed in dark lairs, it was Christ that gave them their terrible strength, and it was Christ alone that they feared. When the first man, Adam, was formed from humble dust, and the first woman, Eve, was formed from her husband's rib, it was Christ Jesus who breathed his mighty breath into their lungs and made them live!

That first page of your Bible has Jesus all over it! His handiwork and his power both created and sustain all things. Your mind should forever weld the great truth of the New Testament Christ to the wonder of creation. Jesus is no foreigner to conception, but with great care knits the bones of the child together. Neither is Christ absent in the manufacturing of all that is formed of water, fire, earth and wind. It is no accident that when John sought to put into record the testimony of Christ he begins with these words: "In the beginning was the Word, and the Word was with God, and the Word was God" (2). You may wish to stop and ask how we can know that this passage should even be compared to that first line of our Holy Bible, and the answer is clear: "All things came into being through him, and apart from him nothing came into being that has come into being" (3). Again we see that "He was in the world, and the world was made through him" (4).

Jesus, called "the Word of God", had been with God from the beginning and by his words, brought forth creation. Let us not teach our children about Christ only when we open up to Matthew, but let us say to them that from eternity past there was a Savior and that by his hand he formed the world and all that is in it! In the beginning God (who was Christ Jesus the historical, present, and future Savior of the world) made the heavens and the earth, and all that is within them; and they persist only because he holds them together.

> He is the image of the invisible God, the first-born of all creation. For by him all things were created, in the heavens and on the earth, visible and invisible, whether thrones or dominions or rulers or authorities—all things have been created through him and for him. He is before all things, and in him all things endure. (5)

Now let me quickly sweep out of the way the cobwebs of deceit and the dirt of false interpretation and throw light rightly upon the phrase "the firstborn of all creation." This is not to say, as some argue, that he was created, for the next verse says he created all things and we already know (from John) that nothing came into being (arose, was made to be, or came upon the stage of history) apart from his (that is, Christ's) power of creation. We must not presume that the sole creator was by some means created, for he has always been. Rather we understand that before there was form of any sort, there was the invisible God, and there was the Spirit, that Holy Ghost whom would soon become our teacher, and there was Christ, singular in form! *Can you imagine it?*

There was no form of any kind, not a mountain, or a pond, not an angel, or a power (save that which rightly belonged to God). There was not so much as a speck of dust; there was only God in his three persons. Of what form he was we do not know. What shape the pre-incarnate Christ took we may never know. But there is something significantly deep in this phrase: "the firstborn of all creation." He is the firstborn heir; the first to receive the Father's blessing; the first to sit upon the throne; the first to be raised to life and the first of those who will be eternally glorified. But make no mistake that he was not created, for the firstborn is the creator of all things.

"For by him all things were created." I love how Paul tells us here that Christ is the creator of not only earthly things but also heavenly things. Christ has created all that the eye perceives and all that the eye shall never behold. The power of Christ formed even the thrones and those who would sit upon them. If there is a ruler or authority it was birthed through the work of Jesus. Is it any wonder then that the seas blowing and beating against a fishing vessel and seeking to drown fearful men would make haste to quiet themselves and rest from their turmoil at the voice of Jesus (6)? The sea knows him who made it. Should we be surprised that water, content to be as much, should in great jars of clay be compelled to become wine at the urging of the one who made all things (7)? Would we stare wide-eyed seeing that the devils tremble before him, he who might cast them into the abyss before their time, and that they would call him LORD seeing that it was Jesus himself who created them and gave them the authority by which they run to and fro, albeit briefly (8)? Do we find ourselves amazed that a tomb four days sealed should be opened and that one previously overcome by death should come out alive (9)? Are we astounded that he whose heart had not pushed blood through veins in ninety-six hours should, with excited obedience, jump to life, and that a brain previously lost to that sleep that closes all men's eyes should come awake with thoughts and power? Yet dead brains and hearts and lifeless muscles do move at the word of their Maker, not in tired, slow jerking motions as though they must relearn their duty but rather in instant power and fullness of skill are they put to work. Is it too marvelous for us to think on the great granite stones, rocks that dot hillsides and river basins, those that make up the face of the mountain, and those that a child may carry in his pocket, should cry out in praise and worship of Jesus if all human tongues should be silenced (10)? They would do such a thing because they know him who formed them and made them long ago. I cannot even begin to guess here at the wonder of the heavens, but I can say that whether earthly or heavenly, visible or invisible, whatever throne or dominion, ruler or authority, all were made by Jesus Christ. All things were made by his power. Ultimately all things which were made by him were also made for him.

"For us there is one God, the Father, from whom are all things and we exist for him; and one LORD, Jesus Christ, by whom are all things, and we exist through him" (11). It is great news to us that the Bible tells us over and over again that all things have come by Christ. We see by this passage that not only did he make us but also our existence is through him. We endure and are held together by the power and the wonder of the Creator (12).

As I am typing this, I am looking out my tiny window on a tiny airplane bound for Florida. A river far below me crawls back and forth through the trees. Far to my left is a great floor of billowy clouds, and just ahead seems to be a large cloudbank that we will soon slice through without leaving a mark or sign that we were there. In the stillness of this moment I am compelled to revisit the wonder of creation that God has allowed me to see. I stood in awe of a great Indonesian volcano, spewing forth its white smoke to be certain that it is not forgotten and was struck by God's power. Once, when the cool air of the Himalayan foothills kissed my cheek and the lush green mountains pierced the velvet clouds that blanketed them, I was overwhelmed by the peace my God gives. Chasing wild peacocks across the rice fields in India and stopping by a pond to watch hundreds of silver fish jump in a uniform ballet back and forth reminds me that even these creatures move to the tune of God's glory. Terrified as I hung by a rope over the sheer cliffs of the Carolina mountains and quite frozen in my ascent to the top I found comfort in God, the rock of my salvation. Worshiping my Savior on the beaches of Spain with a small group of fellow believers captured my heart that my God was at work there too. As the fields in Italy raced passed my train window I found myself contemplating the God who knew each blade of grass intimately. I'll never forget the river in Canada that pushed our raft forward and threw us headlong into its mighty current. It forces me to think on Jesus who is my powerful river of life. I would run out of time if I told you of how God has stirred my heart up for him through swaying trees in Oregon trails, and the corals in Hawaii, or how he moved me to silence as I sailed over the blue waters in the Bahamas. How can we see the meteor showers where thousands of fiery darts cut the night sky, or the thunderhead awash with lightning bolts and not be overcome by God's majesty? If we put together a list of the places every eye has fallen on in the course of human history we would not have even touched the edge of all that our Savior has formed. I cannot say it better than the word of God so I give you Job 26:7–14:

> He stretches out the north over empty space and hangs the earth on nothing. He wraps up the waters in His clouds, and the cloud does not burst under them. He obscures the face of the full moon and spreads his cloud over it. He has

inscribed a circle on the surface of the waters at the boundary of light and darkness. The pillars of heaven tremble and are amazed at his rebuke... Behold, these are the fringes of his ways; and how faint a word we hear of him! But his mighty thunder, who can understand?

All that we see of creation and all that we know of this world are nothing more than the fringes of his ways. Another translation says the "hem" of his ways. What a great and mighty Savior we serve! How beautiful he is! How powerful and lovely! When you read the creation account, be certain that you think on him who saves us by his blood, for he is first of all Creator, then Sustainer, and finally Savior and Judge. We only hear a faint whisper and only see a small shadow of all he is and all that he has done. There is not one among us who has understood the mighty thunder of our Jesus, but I guess that is something we can look forward to when we see him face to face.

"In the beginning God (that is Jesus Christ) created the heavens and the earth."

Scripture Index for Chapter One

1. Genesis 1:1 "In the beginning God created the heavens and the earth."

2. John 1:1 "In the beginning was the Word, and the Word was with God, and the Word was God."

3. John 1:3 "All things came into being through him, and apart from him nothing came into being that has come into being."

4. John 1:10 "He was in the world, and the world was made through him, and the world did not know him."

5. Colossians 1:15–17 "He is the image of the invisible God, the firstborn of all creation. For by him all things were created, both in the heavens and on the earth, visible and invisible, whether thrones or dominions or rulers or authorities—all things have been created through him and for him. He is before all things, and in him all things hold together."

6. Mark 4:39 "And he got up and rebuked the wind and said to the sea, 'Hush, be still.' And the wind died down and it became perfectly calm."

7. John 2:7–11 "Jesus said to them, 'Fill the water pots with water.' So they filled them up to the brim. And he said to them, 'Draw some out now and take it to the headwaiter.' So they

took it to him. When the headwaiter tasted the water, which had become wine, and did not know where it came from (but the servants who had drawn the water knew)…This beginning of his signs Jesus did in Cana of Galilee, and manifested his glory, and his disciples believed him."

8. Matthew 8:28–32 "When he came to the other side into the country of the Gadarenes, two men who were demon-possessed met him as they were coming out of the tombs. They were so extremely violent that no one could pass that way. And they cried out, saying, 'What business do we have with each other, Sod of God? Have you come here to torment us before the time?' Now there was a herd of many swine feeding at a distance from them. The demons began to entreat him, saying, 'If you are going to cast us out, send us into the herd of swine.' And he said to them, 'Go.'"

9. John 11: 41–44 "so they removed the stone. Then Jesus raised his eyes, and said, 'Father, I thank you that you have heard me. I knew that you always hear me; but because of the people standing around I said it, so that they may believe that you sent me.' When he had said these things, he cried out with a loud voice, 'Lazarus, come forth.' The man who had died came forth, bound hand and foot with wrappings, and his face was wrapped around with a

cloth. Jesus said to them, 'Unbind him, and let him go.'"

10. Luke 19:40 "But Jesus answered, 'I tell you, if these become silent, the stones will cry out!'"

11. 1 Corinthians 8:6 "Yet for us there is but one God, the Father, from whom are all things and we exist for Him; and one LORD, Jesus Christ, by whom are all things, and we exist through Him."

12. Colossians 1:17 "He is before all things, and in Him all things hold together."

GENESIS 3:

The Grand Entrance of Death and Grace

The stage had been set, and it seemed all the players were in their places as the curtain went up. God had laid a beautiful backdrop of a garden lush with life, and Adam and his wife enjoyed not only the pristine wonder of it all, but also the walks in the cool of the day with their Creator. It seemed all too perfect; there was but one law: "From the tree of the knowledge of good and evil you shall not eat, for in the day that you eat from it you will surely die," and certainly that would be a simple enough law by which to abide (Genesis 2:17).

Then the antagonist enters. Satan, the crafty serpent of old, makes his move into our unspoiled play, and you can almost feel the tensions rise. If there had been a musical score to this third chapter of Genesis it would have most certainly been ominous and dark, building a crescendo of chills up and down the spine of those who would hear it. His goal, though a simple one, was foul and violent, for he desired nothing more than to "steal, kill, and destroy" all that God had made (1). He was resolute, and he was crafty. He knew the law, and if he could but draw these two fine creations of the Holy God into sin, he knew that the God who does not lie (2) must fulfill the promise of judgment and the swift penalty of death.

So it happened that Eve was deceived, and in turn she saw her husband, Adam, rebel against the command of God and the dark fog of sin set in upon the hearts of mankind, ushering in death for all time. Satan must have been pleased with himself as the two slunk away in fear and shame, doing their very best to cover their sin so that perhaps God would not take notice of their nakedness (3).

God had said that in the day they ate of the tree they would surely die. It is true that the shadow of death fell across the world, and creation, which had been made to endure, now felt the icy hand of the grave. There wouldn't be anything that would escape the grip of death. But the fear that must have overwhelmed these two sinners was the word of God that still hung in their ears. "In the day that you eat of it you shall surely die." Little did they know that what would happen in the next few moments would set the tone for the course of human history and that instead of wrath being poured out it was mercy that was due to be unleashed.

Adam and Eve, naked and ashamed, have fashioned clothes for themselves from fig leaves and have hidden themselves from God for they heard him as he came walking in the garden. He was seeking his creation and sin had them hiding, for the penalty of this sin was greater than they could bear.

"Where are you?" came the voice of God into the stillness of the garden (4). Adam's heart must have been raging in his chest. He knew it was vain to hide. When he came face to face with God and the sin was exposed all the players were present. Center stage stood the Holy Righteous One, and before him the adversary, Satan, and the newly fallen, Adam and Eve. It was time for the sentence to be handed down. The basics were covered: a curse had fallen upon creation, a curse so vile that the whole of the world would groan and long for the redemption it would one day find in the coming of the Savior (5).

But then something strange happened. In that moment when the just Judge should have fulfilled his word against Adam and Eve, he didn't! In that moment when *their* blood should have been shed for *their* sin, it wasn't! God moved past the two lawbreakers and found an animal. We don't know what type it was, but if the rest of the Bible is any indication, we could offer some sort of guess. Still the Bible tells us "The LORD God made garments of skin for Adam and his wife, and clothed them" (6). God saw the covering that Adam and Eve had provided for themselves, and as if to say, "Fig leaves won't cover your sin, I must make a covering suitable for your sin," he took the life of an animal. It was the first time anything had ever died, and it must have been brutally offensive to the two who witnessed it. Never before had blood been spilled upon the ground. Never before had something faced the fearful throes of death. It must have instilled terror in the otherwise tranquil minds of Adam and Eve, but God had said that they would die on the day they ate, so certainly it was better to have something die in their place, violent though it was, if it meant that God would show them mercy. God then took the flesh of this first sacrifice and covered Adam and Eve. Only the covering for sin that he provided would satisfy his righteous requirements. They would wear the bloody body, the mangled flesh of this one who died in their place, and God would be satisfied that their sin was covered. So our great play comes to a close with death having made a great attack, but grace came also and was a stronger warrior than death would prove to be.

This is not some fairy tale or some archaic story passed down through generations to inspire or to threaten. This is the first picture that God would paint to show the plan he had formed before the foundation of the world. God would begin here in this garden with these two fallen ones to show the purpose of the ages. He would show here that he had always intended to redeem his fallen creatures. What we know now in hindsight is that he always intended to redeem his creation through Christ Jesus (7, 8).

I have wondered often, if I had been there instead of Adam, how long could I have gone without eating from the tree? It is likely that I would have been quick to sin, but the truth is that anyone of us could have been there and the result would have been the same. There is not one among all the peoples of the earth who have remained free from sin. We have all fallen short of the beautiful glory of God, which we were created to exemplify (9). The penalty for that sin in the garden was death and so it remains true today (10). There has not been a single person that has been righteous, good, or seeking after God. We are all ungodly sinners who have been God's enemies since the Garden of Eden (11, 12). It seems, then, that if we are to appear before the just Judge of the earth, our position is a dangerous one. So we hide in shame, and we seek to make coverings for our sin. Think about it for a moment and you can likely pinpoint a time in your life that you have covered up your sin in the presence of your friends, your family, or your loved ones. How often have we hidden ourselves knowing that our sin and shame would be obvious should we come face to face with our Lord?

Now this is where you really need to hear me. There is no covering that you can provide for your sin that will satisfy God's holy requirements. Sin deserves death! We all deserve death! We have sinned against the Living God. I know what you're thinking as you sit there hoping that your "good" deeds will outweigh your bad, but God doesn't view us based on a sliding scale or examine our works in a balance. One day our God will come back to this earth and he will say, "Where are you?" I've heard it hundreds of times in my life: "I'm pretty good, I'm sure God will let me into heaven." But I say to you again that we deserve the full wrath of God for the sins in our lives. Adam and Eve deserved death! There was but one law and they broke it! But God had an eternal purpose he was about to put into effect.

There was a moment when Adam came out from his hiding place and stood before the Merciful God. There was that moment when God had to fulfill his violent judgment according to the word he had spoken. In that moment God made a sacrifice in place of those who deserved to die and so it is for us. We, the wretched sinners, find that "while we were still helpless, at the right time, Christ [Jesus] died for the ungodly" (Romans 5:6).

Adam and Eve didn't deserve that grace!

We don't deserve Christ!

We deserve to die, but we don't have to because Jesus died for us!

Think about it in terms of the garden again. You and I are the ones there in the cool shadows of the evening. You and I are the ones called to obedience. You and I are the ones all too captivated by the sinful desires within us. You and I are the ones that put out our hands and took hold of that which God had forbidden. You and I felt the sting of shame as we were wrapped in the dark blanket of guilt. You and I were overcome by the fearful expectation of the wrath and fury of God. You and I ran from him who is holy and just. It is quite a terrifying scene, but we must not stay hidden. We must not leave off here. We must finish the play.

God beckons us from our hiding place. Oh, the sweetness of God to draw us out of our shame! Still we approach tentatively, fully expecting his heavy hand to fall on us and to scatter us like powder. But then comes the miracle of grace as God moves past us, the ones worthy of death, and takes the One who had committed no sin and lays our sin, *my sin,* on him (13). He canceled the debt of sin by nailing it to the cross and removed the curse *from* us by becoming the curse *for* us (14, 15). Jesus took the wrath we deserved and bore it in his body on the cross (16, 17)! Jesus didn't simply take away our debt. Jesus *became* our sin, *became* our curse and *bore* the full measure of God's wrath! I was supposed to be the "cursed one of God," but Jesus took the curse in my stead. I owed the great debt of death for my sin, but it was Jesus who paid the costly price with his blood. I should have been crushed under the raging fury of the fullness of God's wrath, yet it was Jesus the Christ who was forsaken by his Father and put on my wrath like a garment.

In the same way that Adam and Eve had their sin covered by the sacrifice God made in the Garden of Eden, we find that it is the sacrifice of God's "only begotten Son" that covers our sin now. Now we are blessed, because if we are covered by Jesus' blood then we are forgiven and instead of death we find that we are given beautiful eternal life (18, 19)

God provided the first covering for sin, and it was bloody, violent, and gruesome—but it was necessary. The last covering for sin was provided by God, but this time it was not a lowly creation, this time it would be his high and holy Son. This time the Creator (see chapter one) would have to die. His death was infinitely more gruesome than that lone animal slain in the garden, but it was necessary. The animal covered, only in part, the sin of the two who had fallen so far, but the blood of Christ releases us all from our sin forever and brings us near to God (20, 21).

Can you see how clearly we can see God's plan of redemption in this third chapter of Genesis? God was pleased to crush his Son for the sake of his glory in redeeming us (22). We must put on Christ! We can no longer come before God in these flimsy, fig leaf coverings we have so often used to hide our sin. We can no longer remain in the shadows of sin under the fearful expectation of God's wrath. He has slain the Holy Lamb of God. It was brutally offensive, but in it is our salvation. We can be created anew. Our old self, stained with sin and worthy of death, is done away with and now we are made new (23).

It makes no matter how vile your sin has been, come to God and let him clothe you and you shall be pure as snow (24).

The purpose of the ages was revealed in the Garden of Eden and fulfilled in Jesus on the cross!

This is but the first thing that points to redemption through Jesus.

Scripture Index for Chapter Two

1. John 10:10 "The thief comes to steal, kill and destroy, but I have come that you might have life and have it to the full."

2. Numbers 23:19 "God is not a man, that He should lie, nor a son of man, that He should repent; has He said, and will He not do it? Or has He spoken, and will He not make it good?"

3. Genesis 3:7–8 "Then the eyes of both of them were opened, and they knew that they were naked; and they sewed fig leaves together and made themselves loin coverings. They heard the sound of the Lord God walking in the garden in the cool of the day, and the man and his wife hid themselves from the presence of the Lord God among the trees of the garden."

4. Genesis 3:9 "Then the Lord God called to the man, and said to him, 'Where are you?'"

5. Romans 8:18–23 "… For the anxious longing of the creation waits eagerly for the revealing of the sons of God. For the creation was subjected to futility, not willingly, but because of Him who subjected it, in hope that the creation itself also will be set free from its slavery to corruption into the freedom of the glory of the children of God. For we know that the whole creation groans and suffers the pains

of childbirth until now. And not only this, but also we ourselves, having the first fruits of the Spirit, even we ourselves groan within ourselves, waiting eagerly for our adoption as sons, the redemption of our body."

6. Genesis 3:21 "The LORD God made garments of skin for Adam and his wife, and clothed them."

7. Ephesians 3:10–11 "…This was in accordance with the eternal purpose which [God] carried out in Christ Jesus our LORD."

8. 2 Timothy 1:8, 9 "…God saved us and called us with a holy calling, not according to our works, but according to His own purpose and grace which was granted us in Christ Jesus from all eternity."

9. Romans 3:23 "For all have sinned and fallen short of the glory of God."

10. Romans 6:23 "For the wages of sin is death, but the free gift of God is eternal life through Christ Jesus our LORD."

11. Romans 3:10–12 "There is none righteous, not even one; there is none who understands, there is none who seeks for God; all have turned aside, together they have become useless; there is none who does good, there is not even one."

12. Romans 5: 6, 8, 10 "For while we were still helpless, at the right time Christ died for the

ungodly. But God demonstrates His own love toward us, in that while we were yet sinners, Christ died for us. For if while we were enemies we were reconciled to God through the death of His Son, much more, having been reconciled, we shall be saved by His life."

13. 2 Corinthians 5:21 "God made Him who knew no sin to be sin on our behalf, so that we might become the righteousness of God in Him."

14. Colossians 2:13, 14 "When you were dead in your transgressions and the uncircumcision of your flesh, He made you alive together with Him, having forgiven us all our transgressions, having canceled out the certificate of debt consisting of decrees against us, which was hostile to us; and He has taken it out of the way, having nailed it to the cross."

15. Galatians 3:13 "Christ redeemed us from the curse of the Law, having become a curse for us—for it is written, 'Cursed is everyone who hangs on a tree'"

16. Romans 5:9 "Much more then, having now been justified by His blood, we shall be saved from the wrath of God through Him."

17. 1 Thessalonians 1:10 "Jesus rescues us from the wrath to come."

18. Romans 4:7 "Blessed are those whose lawless deeds have been forgiven, and whose sins have been covered."

19. John 3:16 "For God so loved the world that He gave His only begotten son that whosoever believeth in Him shall not perish but have everlasting life."

20. Revelation 1:5 "Jesus Christ, the faithful witness, the firstborn of the dead, and the ruler of the kings of the earth. To Him who loves us and released us from our sins by His blood."

21. Ephesians 2:13 "But now in Christ Jesus you who formerly were far off have been brought near by the blood of Christ."

22. Isaiah 53:10–12 "But the LORD was pleased to crush Him, putting Him to grief; if He would render Himself as a guilt offering... He poured out Himself to death, and was numbered with the transgressors; yet he himself bore the sin of many, and interceded for the transgressors."

23. 2 Corinthians 5:17 "Therefore if anyone is in Christ, he is a new creature; the old things passed away; behold, new things have come."

24. Isaiah 1:18 "Come now, and let us reason together. Though your sins are as scarlet, they will be as white as snow; though they are red like crimson, they will be like wool."

GENESIS 7:

The Ark of Salvation

God looked upon the people of the earth and was grieved deeply in his heart. The earth had become corrupt and was filled with all manners of violence (1). These were the ones he had formed from the dust. He had knit these very souls together. But even as God was sorrowful, he found his justice stirred up. He knew as he looked over the earth that he could not abide with the wickedness of the human heart forever. There in the shadows of heaven stood Wrath and Judgment. They were a brutal pair. They were holy. They were righteous. They were the friends and neighbors of Love and Mercy in the very character of God. Yet their purpose was more formidable than their softer brothers. Wrath and Judgment waited for the command of God.

"Not yet," came the word of God. "We will give them 120 years and then we will blot them out. We will blot out those we have created" (2). Wrath and Judgment took their weapons in hand and waited. One hundred and twenty years would pass in a breath.

When they had stepped to the side, God, deeply moved, beckoned Love and Mercy near his throne: "Do you see the man called Noah? He has found favor in my sight. He alone is righteous and so we shall spare him and his family from the wrath I am about to pour out. I shall hold back, with my righteous right hand, Wrath and Judgment until I have first shown Love and Mercy to him."

One evening as righteous Noah was keeping his crop, the LORD God spoke to him with Love and Mercy, "Noah."

"Yes, LORD?"

"The earth is so filled with violence that the end of all flesh has come before me; and behold, I am about to destroy them and the earth." God didn't stop speaking there but in that pause that takes hold of the space between a period and the beginning of the next sentence, in the pause between the ticking hands of the clock, Noah's heart sank. Fear bathed him with trembling. But God continued, "Make for yourself an ark for you and your sons and your respective wives. I will bring a flood of water upon the earth, to destroy all flesh. But you and yours I shall save because you are righteous and blameless and have walked with me" (3).

Noah's mind reeled within him, but the next morning he resolutely put his hand to the task of building a large boat that would bring salvation to his household and to all the kinds of animals that lived upon the earth.

Let the reader imagine how his days must have passed.

The first day, he prayed and walked off the length and width of the great ark that would save.

The people mocked him.

The second day he enlisted his sons to put their shoulders to the work.

The people mocked him.

The third day he worked his hands to blisters.

The people mocked him.

The fourth day found great drops of water bursting from his brow.

The people mocked him.

The fifth day his hands bled and his muscles ached.

The people mocked him.

The sixth day bruises set in on tender joints.

The people mocked him.

The seventh day he wept at the overwhelming task.

The people mocked him.

On day 21, 600* (4) he stood back from the labor. He was finished! The work was done! It had only taken sixty years. And the people continued to mock.

†

When the work of the ark had been completed and found whole, God spoke to Noah again: "Enter the ark, you and all your household" (5).

So Noah and his family entered the ark at the word of the LORD. Their faith had overcome their anxiety and would prove to be their salvation (6).

The next seven days passed with much hustle and commotion as the region surrounding the ark was filled with a multitude of creatures great and small. Birds flocked in every color to the ark and called it home. The great elephant lumbered slowly up and into the ark. Lions roared with knowledge of the coming judgment. Horses came and stamped the ground. The hare nervously chewed a stalk of grass as she sniffed about. The opossum thought of playing dead. The rhinoceros shoved with the shoulder to get a better place in line. The giraffe looked timidly over the assembly gathered there. The crocodile smiled at the gazelle that stood nearby. For this journey they would be friends. The small mouse scurried hastily between feet to find a place less dangerous to stand. The platypus stood toward the back wishing not to be teased. The snail melted away as he moved patiently forward. The desert lizard had arrived early and found a place among the rafters. The grizzly found himself more agitated than normal. The tiny ant got everyone in single file. This was quite a conglomeration, and the lines of the beasts stretched out to the edge of the world it seemed. They continued coming until the ark was filled.

The multitude of creatures and the eight souls waited.

On the seventh day, the great door of the ark was

lifted into place and the zoo along with its keepers were sealed inside. God had shut them in. He was determined to save these (7).

Wrath and Judgment had been waiting for this moment and they waited with agitated anticipation. God's fury was about to be poured out with the fierceness of a hurricane.

On the seventeenth day of the second month, God ceased to hold back Wrath and Judgment, and the floodwaters came upon the earth. Wrath opened the great floodgates in heaven and water spilled down in sheets. Judgment dove into the deep places of the seas and struck them such that they burst open and water shot up from those dark recesses (8). The tsunami of God's fierce power swept over the land. Those who had mocked these many years were now pale with fright. The waters ran like a great army from the high places of the earth to the low places. Once the valleys had been filled and overcome the waters sought to cover the hills. They were an easy conquest and had been defeated in a matter of days. But the great waters would not be content until they had topped the mountains. Meanwhile, the people of the earth had retreated. They found themselves too weak to stand against the onslaught of God's wrath. No sword could stand. No spear could pierce this untiring foe. Their final stand was on the mountaintops. They had lost a great many of their number in the valleys and the hills. Those who had been too feeble to climb had fallen easily. People clambered over each other, pulling and pushing with a blatant disregard for safety. Yet the waters rose further, undeterred by the cries and screams from the duty of destruction that lay before them.

The waters prevailed.

The mountains were overcome.

Those who had filled the heart of God with sorrow for their great wickedness had been cast down. There was not a place on earth that the judgment of God had not found. He had filled every crevice and every pit. There was no safe haven. There was no victory. There was no salvation.

Except in the ark.

Far across the sea of water, pitching back and forth on the waves, the ark had been lifted up and exalted above the earth. There, inside that perfect form, eight souls had been saved while the rest of the world had been condemned. The Lord had not lied! His judgment and wrath had been poured out. But God had commanded that an ark be built for the purpose of salvation. He had sealed them within the ark. Because of God's great mercy, these had been saved!

Forty days later, God, with his wrath fully satisfied, shut up the gates he had opened in heaven and the water ceased to run forth from the sky. He took the fountains of the deep that had spewed forth torrents and closed them. And all was quiet. The wicked had been removed.

God remembered Noah and all who were with him on the ark and caused a wind to pass over the earth. It ran from wave to wave, submitting the water to its powerful blowing and the water began to subside (9).

Finally, on the twenty-seventh day of the second month God called to Noah again, "Go out of the ark. You and all that are living with you." It had been a year and ten days. The ark had not only saved Noah and his family but had carried him to a new earth. The wicked had been wiped away and the earth stood renewed and fresh. (10)

God had seen man's wickedness. He had determined to put them to death. He had prepared an ark for their salvation. He waited with great patience. He had sealed the righteous in the ark. He had poured out his fury on the wicked. He had rescued the holy ones. He carried them to a new earth.

†

So here we are upon this earth, still wicked at heart, still denying the God who formed us. He has already determined not to bear our contempt forever. He is holding back his wrath and judgment until they should be released in that certain hour and day and month and year. Destruction will fall so swiftly upon us for our sin that we will be drowned in our guilt. Fleeing the coming wrath will not create victory for us. Valleys and hills and mountains will not cover us or offer us any sanctuary. If our eyes would be opened, we would see the divine countdown. Every minute that passes draws us nearer to the day of God's vengeance and to the hour of salvation (11).

Men are bloodying their hands and bruising their muscles to see their own souls saved. Great drops of sweat are pouring over furrowed brows in futile endeavors to be redeemed. They think vain thoughts of rescuing themselves and preserving their own. But they will all fail.

Give up your worthless efforts at salvation, o man! Should you labor thirty years, or one hundred, and bend your back to the work, still you would have fallen short. Even if you enlist the help of family and friends you will find that you have not made any progress in your salvation.

But there is hope.

There is salvation even now from the hour of God's fury.

Look there! His name is Jesus the Christ! He is the one who has formed you!

With a prayer upon his lips, he sweat great drops of blood in your place (12). He resolutely put his shoulder to the task of dying. His hands bled from the nails that held him to the cross. His joints were bruised from the beating he had endured. His muscles were stiff and sore from having borne the cross. The mocking fell on him more violently than the whip that had flayed the flesh from his back. Then, as the wicked crowd looked on, he cried out with a loud voice, "It is finished!" (13).

Do you see that bloodied man on the cross? He is your ark! There is salvation in no one else! (14) There is no other way to be spared from the coming judgment. Come to him you who are weak and weary. Those of you who are laden down with sins come and find your rest in the Christ (15)!

The storm clouds have gathered on the horizon. The armies have gathered at the city gate. The wild beasts have encircled you. The vultures have gathered for the coming onslaught. The floodwaters have filled your lungs and plunged you deep beneath the surface.

But it isn't too late. There is room yet in the ark for you! The door remains open. Christ has prepared his body to be your salvation. The faith that saved Noah shall save you.

You find yourself wondering if you will be safe there. Take courage, fellow sinner! God is the one who shuts the door! God is the one who seals us in the great and holy ark of salvation! Your soul will not be lost there (16).

If there were no coming flood there would be no need for an ark. If the flood comes but the ark is imperfect then we should all be lost despite our faith. If the flood comes and the ark is perfect but you do not hide yourself therein, then you shall be overcome by God.

There is a coming flood. There is a perfect ark that has been prepared for you. The door yet stands open. Run for it! Hasten to it!

There inside you are safe and saved, unable to be drowned in the torrent, for God has made you secure. Find peace there. Find yourself exalted and lifted up from the death and decay of the world. Just as Noah and his were lifted up above the corpse-saturated waters of a vile earth so shall we be lifted up from death and decay (17). As Noah was carried to a new

earth, fresh and full of new life, so shall we be trans-
ferred from this lowly world to a high and holy one.

Jesus is your ark of salvation. Rest your blistered
hands. Your labor cannot save you. The ark is God's
gift for you. By faith you shall come.

God has seen man's wickedness. He has determined to put them to death. He has prepared an ark
for their salvation. He is waiting with great patience.
He has sealed the righteous in the ark. He will pour
out his fury on the wicked. He will rescue the holy
ones. He will carry them to a new earth (18).

Scripture Index for Chapter Three

1. Genesis 6:6 "The LORD was sorry that he had made man on the earth, and he was grieved in his heart."

2. Genesis 6:3 "Then the LORD said, 'My Spirit shall not strive with man forever, because he also is flesh; nevertheless his days shall be numbered at one hundred and twenty years.'" [Author Note: Some say that when God numbered men's days at 120 years that was to say that no one would live longer than 120 years from that point forward. The bible does not support this or agree with it. Based on Genesis 11, we see that Shem lived to be 600, Arpachshad lived to be 438, Shelah lived to be 433, Eber lived to be 464, Peleg lived to be 239, Reu lived to be 302, and Abraham would live to be 175 (Genesis 25:7). In the twentieth century, a woman lived to be 122 years and 164 days old. The point is that for hundreds of years people lived more than 120 years and sometimes still do. It is my contention that when God said he would only contend with men for 120 years that was to say that a countdown had begun until the flood would end men's lives on the earth. So, God sees men's wicked hearts. He is grieved. He decides to flood the earth, and somewhere between thirty and ninety years later he instructs Noah to build an ark.

3. Genesis 6:13–14, 17–18 "Then God said to Noah, 'The end of all flesh has come before me; for the earth is filled with violence because of them; and behold, I am about to destroy them with the earth. Make for yourself an ark of gopher wood. Behold, I, even I am bringing the flood of water upon the earth, to destroy all flesh in which is the breath of life, from under heaven; everything that is on the earth shall perish. But I will establish my covenant with you; and you shall enter the ark."

4. We know that around the time Noah was 500 he had all three of his sons: "Noah was five hundred years old, and Noah became the father of Shem, Ham, and Japheth" (Genesis 5:32). We also know that Noah was 600 when the flood came on the earth: "Noah was six hundred years old when the flood of water came on the earth" (Genesis 7:6). We further know that when God tells Noah to build an ark Noah's three sons were already married and yet without children: "You shall enter the ark—you and your sons and your wife, and your son's wives with you" (Genesis 6:18). (There is the possibility that when God first came to Noah the boys were still youths and unmarried and that God is speaking of the future wives of the boys but we can't be certain.) The Bible isn't as specific here as we would like it to be. We know that in actuality Shem (one of Noah's sons) was ninety-eight when the flood

started (Genesis 11:10) and didn't have his first son until two years after the flood. (Meaning Shem was born when Noah was 502. He is the only son whose age we know for certain.) It is safe to assume that Shem is the oldest as he is always given preeminence when mentioned with his brothers. With that in mind we come to understand that Noah didn't have all three sons by the time he turned 500, but rather "Noah who was about 500 had three sons, Shem, Ham, and Japheth." It is not unlike people who are about to turn thirty-four in a month or two to say they are "Thirty-four. Well, almost." We are talking about people who lived for centuries at a time. It is reasonable that Moses, as he recorded this book, instead of saying, "Noah had Shem when he was 502, Ham when he was 503, and Japheth when he was 505," to simplify said, "Noah was 500 and *became* the father of Shem, Ham, and Japheth" (Emphasis added). Notice the word "became." The reason that I had Noah building the ark for sixty years is because it is not unheard of for the men in the Bible to be married around forty years of age. (Isaac was at least thirty-seven. Esau was forty. His brother Jacob was older.) Honestly, Noah could have been building the ark closer to ninety years, or maybe it was more like thirty or forty years. Any way you slice it, it was a long time to work on an ark and to be subjected to ridicule.

5. Genesis 7:7 "Then Noah and his sons and his wife and his sons' wives with him entered the ark because of the water of the flood."

6. Hebrews 11:7 "By faith Noah, being warned by God about things not yet seen, in reverence prepared an ark for the salvation of his household, by which he condemned the world, and became an heir of the righteousness which is according to faith."

7. Genesis 7:13–16 "On the very day Noah and Shem and Ham and Japheth and their wives entered the ark, so also the beasts after every kind went into the ark. Those that entered, male and female of all flesh, entered as God had commanded him; and the LORD closed [the door] behind him."

8. Genesis 8:1–2, 14 "The fountains of the deep and the floodgates of the sky were closed, and the rain from the sky was restrained. In the 601st year in the second month, on the twenty seventh day of the month, the earth was dry."

9. Genesis 8:1 "But God remembered Noah and all the beasts and all the cattle that were with him in the ark; and God caused a wind to pass over the earth, and the water subsided."

10. Genesis 8:15–16 "Then God spoke to Noah, saying, 'Go out of the ark, you and all that are with you.'"

11. Ezekiel 7:17–19 "All hands will hang limp and all knees will become like water. Shud-

dering will overwhelm them. They will fling their silver into the streets and hate their gold; their silver and gold will not be able to deliver them in the day of the wrath of the LORD." Zepheniah 1:14–18 "Near is the great day of the LORD. A day of wrath is that day, a day of trouble and distress, a day of destruction and desolation, a day of darkness and gloom, a day of clouds and thick darkness. Neither their silver nor their gold will be able to deliver them. On the day of the LORD's wrath; all the earth will be devoured." Romans 2:5 "But because of your stubbornness and unrepentant heart you are storing up wrath for yourself in the day of wrath and revelation of the righteous judgment of God." Revelation 6:16, 17 "They said to the mountains, 'Fall on us and hide us from the presence of him who sits on the throne, and from the wrath of the Lamb'; for the great day of their wrath has come, and who is able to stand?"

12. Luke 22:44 "And being in agony he was praying very fervently; and his sweat became like drops of blood, falling down upon the ground."

13. John 19:30 "Jesus said, 'It is finished!' And he bowed his head and gave up his spirit."

14. Acts 4:12 "There is salvation in no one else; for there is no other name under heaven that has been given among men by which we must be saved."

15. Matthew 11:28–30 "Come to me, all who are weary and heavy-laden, and I will give you rest. Take my yoke upon you and you will find rest for your souls."

16. Ephesians 1:13 "Having also believed, you were sealed in Christ with the Holy Spirit of promise." Ephesians 4:30 "Do not grieve the Holy Spirit of God, by whom you were sealed for the day of redemption."

17. 1 Corinthians 6:14 "Now God has not only raised the LORD, but will also raise us up through his power."

18. 2 Peter 3:3–13 "Mockers will come saying, 'Where is the promise of his coming?' It escapes their notice that by the word of God the heavens and earth existed, and that the world at that time was destroyed, being flooded with water. The present heavens and earth are reserved for fire, kept for the Day of Judgment and the destruction of ungodly men. But according to His promise we are looking for new heavens and a new earth, in which righteousness dwells."

GENESIS 28:

The Ladder Between Heaven and Earth

Jacob ran as far as he could, and then stopped for a moment to rest. But the thoughts of his brother Esau caused him to get up and run again. He would be no match for his brother in this open wilderness. Jacob knew that he was soft, and his brother was a mighty hunter. With a simple twist of his wrist, Esau could break the soft neck of Jacob. This thought caused his feet to press on over the rocks and the sand. His blood was pounding in his ears. Not too long before, Jacob had traded his brother a bowl of soup for the birthright, and just yesterday he had tricked his blind father into giving him the blessing that rightly belonged to Esau. (1) Now the only thing consoling Esau was the thought of killing his brother (2). So Jacob continued to run.

As the sun set in the distance and the shadows fell, so did any hope of redemption. Jacob collapsed to the ground, his body limp from exhaustion, and his feet bloody from the trek. Perhaps it would be best to die. Perhaps he deserved to be caught. He thought of the name his parents had given him and grimaced at the irony of it all (3). His name meant "one who grabs the heel" or "layer of snares," yet it seemed he was the one who had been caught. He pulled a stone to his head and lay down to sleep and perhaps to die (4). It was there in the dark that the tears came and soon he was deep in a fitful sleep.

Then Jacob dreamed a dream!

A ladder was set upon the earth and its very top pierced the clouds and ended in heaven. Angels of God were busy making their way ascending and descending on it. The LORD stood at the top and spoke to Jacob, "I am the God of your fathers, and the land on which you lie I will give to you as an inheritance. Just as I have promised to Abraham and Isaac so now I confirm to you that I will do as I have said. I will be with you and will never forsake you until I have accomplished all that I have said I would do" (5).

When Jacob woke from his dream he was overcome with great fear now realizing that this must be the very house of God, even the very gate of heaven! He took the stone on which he had slept and poured oil on it and renamed the place Bethel, which means "house of God" (6).

If we are not careful we will look past this dream and think of it as nothing more than a moment of teaching and revelation for Jacob, but it is richer by far.

✝

Jesus was walking among the people for the first time not as a carpenter but now as their teacher, their Savior. He had laid down the hammer and the plane and was now teaching the things of his Father who was in heaven.

Andrew was the first to follow Jesus and quickly brought his brother Simon with him. No sooner had Simon met Jesus than Jesus changed his name to Cephas (7). The next day Jesus added Philip to the group, who promptly went to bring his friend Nathanael to Jesus.

"Nathanael," Philip exclaimed, "we have found him of whom Moses wrote about in the Law. Certainly he is the Messiah. It is none but Jesus of Nazareth."

Nathanael scoffed, "Can anything good come from Nazareth?"

"Come and see," Philip said knowingly

Nathanael rose from under the fig tree where he had been enjoying the shade and followed tentatively (8).

As Nathanael approached the small group around Jesus, the teacher spoke indicating Nathanael: "Here is an Israelite in whom nothing is false."

"How do you know me?" Nathanael asked.

"Oh, Nathanael, I knew you even before Philip called you. I saw you sitting under the fig."

Nathanael was surprised by this and thought that Jesus must certainly be the Son of God. He was convinced of it!

"You, Rabbi, are the Son of God and the King of Israel."

The Savior smiled knowingly, "Do you believe because I said, 'I saw you under the fig?' Nathanael, you shall see greater things than these for you shall see the *heavens opened up and the angels of God ascending and descending on the Son of Man*" (9, Emphasis added).

There it was!

In that moment Jesus had interpreted the dream of Jacob. The men gathered around him knew their Bible well. They knew the language. There was no other place in all of Scripture where the heavens were opened up and the angels of God were ascending and descending. The man that stood before them now *was* the Son of God, the King of Israel, the Teacher, and the Savior. This man was the ladder, the only point of contact between heaven and earth. There would be no other way than by this man to enter the doors of heaven. It mattered not if you were "a layer of snares." It mattered not what you were running from. Here was your access point to the things of heaven; here was your ladder that you might depart from the wickedness of this earth and tread where angels have trod!

Oh, sinner, have you grown weary of your running? Does your sin hunt you in the dark? Are you fearful that your name cannot be changed from "enemy" to "friend"? Look! The gate of heaven stands open! You can access it by the Ladder; his name is Jesus! He touches both heaven and earth, and he is your means for salvation.

Scripture Index for Chapter Four

1. Genesis 25:29–34 "When Jacob had cooked stew, Esau came in from the field famished; and Esau said to Jacob, 'Please let me have a swallow of that red stuff there.' But Jacob said, 'First sell me your birthright.' So Jacob gave Esau bread and stew; and Esau despised his birthright." Genesis 27:1–40 "Isaac said to Esau, 'Your brother came deceitfully and has taken away your blessing.'"

2. Genesis 27:42 "Behold your brother Esau is consoling himself concerning you by planning to kill you."

3. Genesis 25:26 "So his name was called Jacob." Genesis 27:36 "Is he not rightly named Jacob, for he has supplanted me these two times? He took away my birthright, and behold, now he has taken away my blessing."

4. Genesis 28:11 "He came to a certain place and spent the night there, because the sun had set; and he took one of the stones of the place and put it under his head, and lay down in that place."

5. Genesis 28:12–15 "He had a dream, and behold, a ladder was set on the earth with its top reaching to heaven; and behold, the angels of God were ascending and descending on it."

6. Genesis 28:18–19 "So Jacob rose early in the morning, and took the stone that he had put under his head and set it up as a pillar and poured oil on its top. He called the name of that place Bethel."

7. John 1:42 "Andrew brought him to Jesus, Jesus looked at him and said, 'You are Simon the son of John; you shall be called Cephas' (which is translated Peter)."

8. John 1:43–46 "Philip found Nathanael and said to him, 'We have found him of whom Moses in the Law and also the Prophets wrote—Jesus of Nazareth.' Nathanael said to him, 'Can any good thing come out of Nazareth?'"

9. John 1: 47–51 "Jesus saw Nathanael coming to him, and said of him, 'Behold, an Israelite indeed, in whom there is no deceit!' Nathanael said to him, 'How do you know me?' Jesus answered, 'Before Philip called you, when you were under the fig tree, I saw you.' Nathanael answered him, 'Rabbi, you are the Son of God; you are the King of Israel.' Jesus answered and said to him, 'Because I said to you that I saw you under the fig tree, do you believe? You will see greater things than these. Truly, truly, I say to you, you will see the heavens opened and the angels of God ascending and descending on the Son of Man.'"

GENESIS 42 AND EXODUS 2:

The Overlooked Deliverer

Joseph looked out of the window of his home over the Egyptian countryside. There was a small part of him that thought it was funny that he had been a prisoner and a slave not too many years ago, and now he was the second most powerful man in the nation (1). Twenty-two years earlier at the age of seventeen, he had gone to meet his brothers in the field with their flocks and they had conspired to kill him (2). Their hatred of him was tremendous! Instead they sold him as a slave, and he had ended up in Egypt. A few years after that, he was falsely accused of a heinous crime and spent time in prison. But at thirty years old, Pharaoh had a dream, and Joseph had interpreted it and now here he was.

There had been seven years of abundance immediately followed by seven years of famine, but Joseph
was wise and the people of Egypt were prepared. Now
here they were two years into the famine and Joseph
was confident that God had sent him to this place to
be the savior of many lives (3).

On this particular morning Joseph kissed his wife
and his two boys good-bye and went down to the silos
to oversee the distribution of the food. Joseph was
pleased that God would use him in such a way. He was
overjoyed at the prospect of being able to give these
people seed and bread so that they might have life.

As the afternoon wore on, Joseph saw many come
and go, but there was a particular group of men that
caught his eye. There were ten of them along with their
camels and servants. They were covered in the dust of
many miles, and their sacks were worn out from the
journey. Each man wore a beard, and each forehead
was darkened by the sun. They had grown up consid-
erably, but there was no doubt about it; these were his
older brothers!

He drew himself up a bit on his seat and spoke to
them through an interpreter so as not to give himself
away (4). He did not wish to speak plainly to them just
yet. He was certain they would not recognize him. He
was only a boy when they had sold him, and now he
was a man, nicely formed and clean-shaven, dressed in
fine clothes, and adorned with many rings.

"You are all spies!" Joseph shouted at them gruffly.
The brothers could see the anger in this man's face
and turned in surprise as the interpreter relayed the
accusation.

"No, my Lord, we are all brothers. We just want some food as we have none in our land," they pleaded with the translator to make their plight known.

"No! Certainly you are all spies sent to see where our land is defenseless!"

As the message was relayed the men began to be fearful. "We are brothers. There were twelve of us. The youngest is at home, and one was torn to pieces by wild animals."

The lie stung Joseph to the heart. He wondered if they ever thought of him or if they had come to believe their own lie.

"Liars! For I know that you are all spies. This is how I can test you. I shall put you all in prison and send one of you for your youngest brother that I may know if you speak the truth." And with that he had them all locked up in prison for three days.

On the third day Joseph had them brought out of prison and spoke to them again through his slave, "I fear God, so if you are honest men I shall let you go so that you may take food to your households, but one of you must stay with me in my prison so that you must return. Certainly you shall not see my face again unless you come with your youngest brother by your side" (5).

The words of this Egyptian ruler fell deep into the hearts of these men, and they became weak in their knees. One of the brothers spoke in a broken voice, "We are guilty concerning our brother Joseph. We saw the distress of his soul as he pleaded and begged us for his life, but we would not listen. Therefore, this great distress and terror has fallen on us."

Reuben answered them, saying, "Did I not tell you, 'Do not sin against the boy'; but you would not listen? Now we must give a reckoning for his blood" (6). As they spoke amongst themselves, they did not realize that their brother was just a few feet away dressed as an Egyptian lord, and he understood their every word. With these last few sentences Joseph felt his heart pricked and turned away from them to weep. He wished that he could show himself to them, but now was not the time (7).

So Simeon was left behind in prison, and the remaining nine brothers returned with their caravan to their father Jacob. The food they brought did little in the way of encouragement, for Jacob had lost another son, this one to an Egyptian ruler (8).

Many months passed, and the food began to grow thin again. There was talk about returning to Egypt for more, but what if the ruler of the land was harsh again? Meanwhile, Simeon anxiously awaited the return of his brothers that he may be rescued, and Joseph awaited the return so he could show himself to his family.

Finally hunger pangs crept upon the household of Jacob and he said to them, "Go back, buy us a little food."

"We can return, father, but only if our youngest brother goes with us." Judah cast a furtive glance downward even as he said it.

Great turmoil ran through the heart of Jacob, but he submitted his son and the nine older brothers made their return to Egypt with their youngest brother in tow.

The days had passed slowly for Joseph as he waited and hoped for the return of his brothers. But one afternoon as he sat on his seat overseeing the distribution of the food, he recognized the clothing and the manners of his brothers in the distance making their way down the street. When he saw that his brother Benjamin was with them he turned to his servant and said, "Bring them to my house and slay an animal for the men to dine with me at noon" (9). Quietly Joseph withdrew to his house ahead of the brothers.

When they were told that they should have lunch with the lord of the land, great fear set in upon the hearts of the brothers. But they were brought in without incident, and they were seated in order of their birth. Their brother Simeon was brought from the prison and seated among them (10).

Joseph greeted the brothers, but moments later having seen his own brother, the son of his mother, he fled the room to weep in great joy and sorrow (11).

The following morning, the brothers, all eleven of them, were given food and sent on their way, but Joseph had laid a trap for them so that they would be brought back before him immediately. When they stood before him they trembled. Each was fearful that his life might be lost. However, Joseph sent his servants away from him, and when the room was silent he brought his brothers near. When they drew close he wept so loudly that all of the Egyptians heard it, and even Pharaoh heard of it. Through his tears and with quaking voice he said, "I am your brother Joseph! I am him who you sold into slavery. Is my father still alive?" (12).

It took a few minutes for the brothers to gather themselves. Once they were convinced this was their brother, fear washed over them like a wave. Joseph was quick to reassure them that he meant them no harm, and that God had brought him to this place to keep them alive. He gave instructions to his brothers to go back to their land and gather all that belonged to them and all the members of their household: "Hurry and come back here to Egypt and I will provide for you and I shall keep you alive" (13).

So the small nation of the Hebrews had been saved. The one whose own people had sold and left for dead had now been revealed as the one who should save them. They had missed it the first time. When they first saw him they were kept from recognizing him, but on this second visit Joseph had made himself known to those who belonged to his family, and they were saved.

†

Moses looked out of the window of his home over the Egyptian countryside. In the distance he could see the Hebrew city. It was the city of the slaves. His heart was deeply stirred within his chest. Those were his people. He knew that it was only by the power of God that he had been spared from death. As an infant, there had been a command that all of the male children of the Hebrews should be cast into the Nile and drowned. But his mother had heard from God and had set him afloat in that same wicked Nile in a basket that his life would be spared (14). He had been found by the Pharaoh's daughter and had been raised as a prince, though many of the royals looked on him with a bitter eye (15).

For close to forty years, he had lived in the household of the Pharaoh and had partaken of his riches and his choice food, but lately the God of his people, his real people, had been speaking to him. He was nervous about the task at hand and hardly understood how God could expect him to be the deliverer of an entire nation of slaves. Why would they listen to him? He sat there in a beautiful room and in lavish robes while they bent their backs before the whips of the taskmasters (16).

With tears in his eyes, but resolution in his step, he determined he would go and live among his own people and suffer as they suffered. Then he could be their deliverer. Then he could save them from slavery! Certainly then they would listen to him and follow his leading (17).

Moses left the comforts of his home and began to endure ill treatment with those who were his own flesh and blood. It wasn't pleasant. It wasn't easy. But it was right! It was necessary if these people were to be saved and brought out of slavery to a land where they could be free. As he bent his back to the work, he kept mumbling over and over under his breath, "This is necessary if they are to be delivered. And I love them, so I shall labor among them."

One afternoon while Moses was walking among his brethren, he saw an Egyptian beating a Hebrew. Having looked this way and that, and finding no one around, he killed the Egyptian and buried his body in the sand. He was certain that the Hebrews would understand that God had sent him to be their deliverer, but they couldn't see it yet.

What he had done was found out, and it was all the motive the Pharaoh needed to finally put to death this Hebrew stain that had for so long sat at his table and eaten his bread. Soldiers were sent to bring Moses back so that he could be condemned for his crimes.

But Moses had fled (18).

Forty years later, Moses found himself married with two sons and living in a land that was not his own. He had been a shepherd of sheep for the whole of that time and was sitting on a rock enjoying the morning sun shining on his face.

It was moments like this when he could see his boys playing in the distance and his lovely wife walking among the tents further down the valley that he almost forgot about all that he had left behind. Still there were echoes that rattled around in his mind. They raised questions like, "Is my brother still living?" and "Did God really tell me that I was to deliver his people? My people?" But as quickly as those thoughts would come they would melt away in a summer breeze or drift away on the lofty clouds. At just that moment when ancient memories were being carried away something on the hillside caught Moses' eye.

A fire!

He jumped to his feet thinking of how to protect the sheep, but then took a second look. There was certainly a fire, but it was limited to a single bush and though the bush blazed, it was not consumed (19). Moses hastened up the hill to see this great sight. As he approached cautiously he could feel the heat of the flame. Just as he was staring in wonder, the voice of God spoke to him from the bush, "Moses, Moses!"

"Here I am," Moses replied, without even feeling foolish for speaking to a bush.

"Do not come closer, but instead remove your sandals, for the place where you stand is holy. I am the God of your father, the God of Abraham, the God of Isaac, and the God of Jacob" (20).

At this Moses hid his face and trembled for he was afraid to look at God.

But God spoke on.

He told Moses that he had not forgotten his people and their cry for help had reached him in heaven: "I have come to deliver them from the power of the Egyptians, and to bring them up to a new land."

The words "deliver them" hung in Moses' ear like a trumpet and shook him to his core. He knew what was coming next.

"Therefore, come now, and I will send you to Pharaoh, so that you may bring my people out of Egypt." God's words cut to the heart of the shepherd.

Moses fought to make all sorts of excuses. He had left that life behind. He had tried before. The people didn't see him as the deliverer (21). The Egyptians would try to kill him. He couldn't speak well. He didn't have any way to prove that he had come from God. Moses hurled excuse after excuse at God, but none of them landed.

"I know you tried before, yet it wasn't the time for them to understand. They'll believe you this time. Your life will not be taken from you. I'll teach you how to speak. I'll clothe you with power and signs so that they will know that you are the deliverer." God had heard excuses before. The pugilists worked away at each other for the better part of the day, but God was victorious.

Moses returned to Egypt.

His brother Aaron was still living and came to his aid. Moses stood before the people of God, his own brothers and sisters, his own nation, and they listened. He showed the signs and power that he had been clothed with from on high, and the people believed. Pharaoh rebelled and was wicked, but this adversary was no match for the great power of God and eventually fell in defeat. Moses led the people forward out of the land of slavery and into a land they could call their own. A new land prepared for them by God.

The great nation of the Hebrews had been saved. One who had been set afloat on the river of death and had been gone for so long a time had now been revealed as the one who should save them. They had missed it the first time. When they first saw him they were kept from recognizing him as their deliverer, but on this second visit Moses had made himself known to those who belonged to his family, and they were saved.

†

Jesus looked from the cross on the hill over the Jerusalem countryside. The shadow of night blanketed the afternoon hours. His people were suffering a famine. This was not a famine for food or drink, but rather for the word of the Lord (22). His people had become hard of heart and deaf in their hearing. They did not know that they were slaves, slaves of the adversary.

Jesus had seen it and longed to feed them. He longed to set them free from slavery. He looked with compassion and sorrow on the people gathered around his bloody nail-pierced feet. Their eyes were full of rage. How cruelly they were oppressed by their taskmaster! How near they were to the door of death for lack of true food and true drink (23)!

He had tried to tell them that he would be their bread. He had tried to let them know that he could set them free indeed (24)! But they would not listen.

They didn't recognize him.

It wasn't the time for them to know him. Not just yet. He had to face death for them. He had to be crucified for their wickedness and for their sins. If they had understood that he had come to save them and deliver them they would have never nailed him to the cross (25). But he had to die in order for them to know him.

He scanned the crowd again and looked over toward the city. He knew his life was slipping away. Every beat of his heart pushed tiny streams of blood from the piercings in his wrists and feet. His head began to feel heavy. "Father, forgive them," he spoke in a whisper (26). It was as though in his final breath he was asking for them to be saved from famine and delivered from slavery. Jesus knew what the end would be. He would not remain dead. They would think that this was the last time they would see him, but they were wrong.

They had rejected their Savior and their Deliverer, but he would come back. He would sit upon his throne, just as Joseph had; he would be clothed with

power from on high, as Moses had been (27). He had
been hidden the first time that he came, but he would
return! And when he did, all those who belonged to
his family, all those who were of his flesh and blood
would finally see him for who he truly was. They may
have overlooked the Deliverer the first time, but when
he comes in glory on the clouds they will know that
he is Savior (28)!

Scripture Index for Chapter Five

1. Genesis 39:4 "Joseph found favor in the sight of Potiphar and became his personal servant." Genesis 39:20 "Potiphar took Joseph and put him into the jail, the place where the king's prisoners were confined; and he was there in the jail." Genesis 41:40–41 "Pharaoh said to Joseph, 'You shall be over my house, and according to your command all my people shall do homage; only in the throne I will be greater than you. See, I have set you over all the land of Egypt.'"

2. Genesis 37:2, 18 "Joseph, when seventeen years of age, was pasturing the flock with his brothers while he was still a youth. When they saw him from a distance and before he came close to them, they plotted against him to put him to death."

3. Genesis 45:5–8; 50:20 "Do not be grieved or angry with yourselves, because you sold me here, for God sent me before you to preserve life. God sent me before you to preserve for you a remnant in the earth, and to keep you alive by a great deliverance. Now, therefore, it was not you who sent me here, but God; and he has made me a father to Pharaoh and Lord of all his household and ruler over all the land of Egypt. As for you, you meant evil against me, but God meant it for good in order to bring about this present result, to preserve many people alive."

4. Genesis 42:23 "They did not know, however, that Joseph understood, for there was an interpreter between them."

5. Genesis 42: 6–20 "Joseph spoke harshly to them. Joseph had recognized his brothers, although they did not recognize him. Joseph said to them, 'You are spies; you have come to look at the undefended parts of our land. It is as I said to you, you are spies; by this you will be tested; by the life of Pharaoh, you shall not go from this place unless your youngest brother comes here.'"

6. Genesis 42:21–22 "They said to one another, 'Truly we are guilty concerning our brother, because we saw the distress of his soul when he pleaded with us, yet we would not listen; therefore this distress has come upon us.' Reuben answered them, saying, 'Did I not tell you, "Do not sin against the boy"; and you would not listen?'"

7. Genesis 42:24 "Joseph turned away from them and wept."

8. Genesis 42:24, 36 "But he took Simeon from them and bound him before their eyes. Then their father Jacob said to them, 'You have bereaved me of my children: Joseph is no more, and Simeon is no more, and you would take Benjamin; all these things are against me.'"

9. Genesis 43:16 "When Joseph saw Benjamin with them, he said to his house steward, 'Bring

the men into the house, and slay an animal and make ready; for the men are to dine with me at noon.'"

10. Genesis 43:33 "Now they were seated before him, the firstborn according to his birthright and the youngest according to his youth, and the men looked at one another in astonishment."

11. Genesis 43:30 "Joseph hurried out for he was deeply stirred over his brother, and he sought a place to weep; and he entered his chamber and wept there."

12. Genesis 45:1, 4 "Then Joseph could not control himself before all those who stood by him, and he cried, 'Have everyone go out from me.' So there was no man with him when Joseph made himself known to his brothers. Then Joseph said to his brothers, 'Please come closer to me.' And they came closer. And he said, 'I am your brother Joseph, whom you sold into Egypt.'"

13. Genesis 45:9, 19 "Hurry and go up to my father, and say to him, 'Thus says your son Joseph, "God has made me Lord of all Egypt; come down to me, do not delay."' Now you are ordered, 'Do this; take wagons from the land of Egypt for your little ones and for your wives, and bring your father and come. Do not concern your-selves with your goods, for the best of all the land of Egypt is yours.'"

14. Exodus 1:22 "Then Pharaoh commanded all his people, saying, 'Every son who is born you are

to cast into the Nile, and every daughter you are to keep alive.'" Exodus 2:2–3 "The woman bore a son and she hid him for three months. When she could hide him no longer, she got him a wicker basket and covered it over with tar and pitch. She put the child into it and set it among the reeds by the bank of the Nile."

15. Exodus 2:5–10 "The child grew, and she brought him to Pharaoh's daughter and he became her son. And she named him Moses, and said, 'Because I drew him out of the water.'"

16. Acts 7:20–25 "Moses was educated in all the learning of the Egyptians, and he was a man of power in words and deeds. But when he was approaching the age of forty, it entered his mind to visit his brethren, the sons of Israel. And when he saw one of them being treated unjustly, he defended him and took vengeance for the oppressed by striking down the Egyptian. And he supposed that his brethren understood that God was granting them deliverance through him, but they did not understand."

17. Hebrews 11:24–26 "By faith Moses, when he had grown up, refused to be called the son of Pharaoh's daughter, choosing rather to endure ill-treatment with the people of God than to enjoy the passing pleasures of sin, considering the reproach of Christ greater riches than the treasures of Egypt; for he was looking to the reward."

18. Exodus 2:15 "Moses fled from the presence of Pharaoh and settled in the land of Midian, and he sat down by a well."

19. Exodus 3:2–3 "The angel of the Lord appeared to him in a blazing fire from the midst of a bush; and he looked, and behold, the bush was burning with fire, yet the bush was not consumed. So Moses said, 'I must turn aside now and see this marvelous sight.'"

20. Exodus 3:4-4:17 "The Lord said, 'I am the God of your father, the God of Abraham, the God of Isaac, the God of Jacob. I have seen the affliction of my people who are in Egypt, and have given heed to their cry for I am aware of their sufferings. So I have come down to deliver them and to bring them up from that land to a good and spacious land. Therefore, come now, I will send you to Pharaoh, so that you may bring my people, the sons of Israel, out of Egypt.'"

21. Acts 7:23–25 "But when he was approaching the age of forty, it entered his mind to visit his brethren, the sons of Israel. And when he saw one of them being treated unjustly, he defended him and took vengeance for the oppressed by striking down the Egyptian. And he supposed that his brethren understood that God was granting them deliverance through him, but they did not understand."

22. Amos 8:11,12 "'Behold, days are coming,' declares the Lord God, 'When I will send a famine on

the land, not a famine for bread or a thirst for water, but rather for hearing the words of the Lord. People will stagger from sea to sea and from the north to the east; they will go to and fro to seek the word of the Lord, but they will not find it.'"

23. John 6:55 "For my flesh is true food, and my blood is true drink."

24. John 8:36 "So if the Son makes you free, you will be free indeed."

25. 1 Corinthians 2:8 "…the wisdom that none of the rulers of this age has understood; for if they had understood it they would not have crucified the Lord of glory…"

26. Luke 23:34 "But Jesus was saying, 'Father, forgive them; for they do not know what they are doing.'"

27. Hebrews 12:2 "…fixing our eyes on Jesus, the author and perfecter of faith, who for the joy set before him endured the cross, despising the shame, and has sat down at the right hand of the throne of God." Revelation 7:17 "For the Lamb in the center of the throne will be their shepherd"

28. Matthew 24:30 "And then the sign of the Son of Man will appear in the sky, and then all the tribes of the earth will mourn, and they will see the Son of Man coming on the clouds of the sky with power and great glory."

EXODUS 11–12:

The Passover

The slave lifted his trembling hand to the doorpost again brushing the macabre "paint" over the roughly hewn wood. His life had been a hard one. He came from a long line of slavery. So much for being the "people of God" he thought to himself as he dipped the stalk back into the bowl.

As if life hadn't been hard enough, this Moses had returned to Egypt after being gone for forty years and now was spreading rumors about "freedom" and a "Promised Land" that God had waiting for them.

For all of them.

How many were they these days? He wasn't educated enough to even fathom a guess but as he turned and looked over the slave city stretching to the horizon he wondered how this God could possibly deliver them. And if he did, how could he ever expect to see a land flowing with milk and honey?

The warm breeze of the evening stroked his face and felt cool as it brushed past the tear-stained cheeks. Each tear had cut a trail through his dirty face.

It wasn't right to be crying. He was too strong for that. He looked at his worn hands and the hyssop stalk and bowl they held now. He knew this was his only chance. His family's only chance. So he went back to painting. It was easy work, but it wasn't right that his wife should do it. This had to be his job.

The last few months had changed his life. When Moses had come and spoke of God's deliverance, he had scoffed, but now he was rethinking his position. How else would you explain all the…what do you call those horrible things that happened? They were abominations. They were plagues! That's it! Plagues so terrible that every crop among the Egyptians, every herd left in the field had been destroyed. Water had been turned to blood. Blood!

His wide eyes looked to the bowl in his hand as he moved to the other side of the doorpost and a shudder gripped him by the neck.

Then there were the frogs, the flies, the darkness, and the dreadful boils. The Egyptians were beset by many wicked things, and yet the city of the slaves had been untouched. It made him wonder if in fact they really were "God's chosen people" (1)?

But this, this was too much. Still, he was a slave, and he knew how to obey orders so he pressed on, painting the doorframe of his peasant home.

Two weeks ago Moses had spoken to the entire assembly and told them that there was only one plague left. This one would eclipse the previous nine in a violent and dreadful way. Moses had said to begin counting.

"Today is day one," he said. "Fourteen days from now the Most High God will come through Egypt about midnight and strike down the firstborn of every household and every stall in this place. But God will save you and deliver you. Furthermore, the Egyptians will pour out their wealth on you, and instead of hindering you from leaving, they will beg you to go" (2).

It was foolish. Why would their masters let them go free much less ask them to leave? And how exactly would God spare the lowly slaves—these "people of God"?

But Moses had continued, "On day ten, take an unblemished lamb into your house and care for it for four days." It seemed a strange thing to say. What manner of instruction was this? But then it got worse: "On the fourteenth day at twilight you and all of your community shall take the lamb from within your home and slaughter it and take its blood and paint the doorframe of your house. In this manner you shall be saved, for when the LORD passes through the land about midnight he will see the blood on your door and pass over you. And you shall keep your life. But if you disobey, the firstborn of every household shall be under the wrath and judgment of God just as the Egyptians will be" (3).

Asher looked through the tiny window into his house and saw his wife baking the unleavened bread and preparing the herbs (4). Near her sat their first child. She was a beautiful child with long flowing hair. She looked so much like her mother. He bit his lip hard to keep the sob from escaping his throat and daubed the last of the blood on his doorframe. He hoped it was enough. Perhaps he should put more. How could he possibly know if this God whom he had never seen or encountered would see this blood? How could he rest if he was unsure as to whether or not he had met the requirements? He could not stand the thought of losing his daughter. For a moment he forgot that he was a firstborn too. What would come of his wife? She was so beautiful! He could not stand the thought of her being abused and tormented by the slave drivers. He clenched his hands and his knuckles whitened.

The sun was setting. Just a few more hours now.

The supper of the lamb was a silent one. Their neighbors had come to share in this final meal since neither family was large enough to consume an entire lamb. The children had cried when he had to kill the lamb. They had loved it being in the house. Being so young the children didn't understand that it was either the lamb's life or theirs, but for the parents it was an easy decision to make. (5)

The fire in the lamps seemed to dance about in an agitated way tonight as the darkness draped across all of Egypt like a heavy curtain. Asher found it difficult to breathe as he began to eat this horrid meal. His wife reached over to touch his hand and the coolness of it caught him by surprise. She was as frightened as he was.

Then came midnight!

The LORD had arrived and brought judgment in his hand!

There was not a home in all of Egypt untouched. The king who sat upon the throne wept over his child, and the prisoner mourned the loss of his firstborn. As lamps were lit from house to house and the dead were found stricken by the very hand of God, the people wept greatly (6).

It started as a scream that pierced the silence of this ominous hour. One Egyptian had found her first-born a victim of God's wrath, and her scream alerted the neighbor and the friend, and eventually the rest of those in the household. From home to home, screams of horror arose as God passed through.

In the slave city, they ate in silence with their staffs in their hands. They were to go quickly. As they waited, they stared at one another by the light of the lamps to see if any should be lost for having not obeyed the word of the LORD. Then it happened! Asher's hair rose on his neck, and his wife gripped his hand more firmly than before. In the distance, they heard a low moan. It was like the howling of a far off wind, but it grew. That, which started as a low moan, grew into a tidal wave of weeping and wailing and surrounded the slave city as all of the inhabitants of a nation mourned at once. Every living voice in every home in Egypt was raised in terror, grief, and despair. The noise was so horrific that such a sound had never been heard before and never should be heard again. The wave of cries crashed over the city as the slaves gathered in their houses and prayed that the blood would be sufficient (7).

And it was!

Moments later, Asher leapt as someone beat on his door. The Egyptians had come to the slave city and were begging them to leave.

"Please go," the terrified man shouted, "lest we all should die at the hand of your God!" So it was everywhere throughout the Hebrew community. Asher looked into the street and saw Egyptians running in panic and laying their riches in the hands of the slaves. The slaves were clinging tightly to their little ones and making their way out of the city (8).

They were free!

God's judgment had come, but he had delivered them. He had seen the blood. He had passed over them. Asher and his family ran from the only home they had ever known. Every painful moment they had spent there flashed before his mind's eye, and he took one final look at the dark doorframe. The blood, the blood of the lamb, had saved their lives.

†

The Teacher lifted his hands up before the men. He held up the bread. It was the Passover celebration. They had celebrated this as a people for thousands of years. This fourteenth day of this first month marked the very day that God had brought his people out of Egypt, out of slavery and bondage, to make their home in the Promised Land. This land. The land he had walked these last few years teaching and preaching. It was customary in this tradition to take up and eat the bread as a symbol of the lamb that their Hebrew ancestors had eaten in that slave village. It was customary to drink the wine as a symbol of the blood that had been painted on the doorframes, the very blood that God had seen, and the very blood that had saved their lives.

The Teacher looked at his students, his disciples. They had learned so much, yet they still did not really understand. They would soon enough, however. This was to be the last night he would walk with them. He looked at each one of them, knowing their hearts, knowing their love for him—or their betrayal—and he found it hard not to weep.

Their eyes were on him to see what great thing he would say this time. They wondered what miracle he might perform. They had seen him walk on water and feed thousands with a few pieces of bread and some fish. They had seen him command demons to depart from tormented souls. Blind had regained sight, and lame had danced. They had even seen the dead walk out of a tomb alive and whole (9).

But this night would lead to the greatest miracle of all. This night would end in the bringing to life of countless souls that had been spiritually dead.

As he lifted up the bread, he spoke, "You have heard that this bread represents the lamb whose blood was spilled so that our ancestors could be set free from slavery, so God in his fury would pass over them. But I tell you that this is *my* body broken for you" (10).

The disciples looked at him puzzled. He always seemed to speak in mysteries. The bread represented the Passover Lamb. How could he say that it was his body?

He held up the cup of wine and spoke again, "This

wine is the new covenant by my blood, which I will pour out for you" (11).

Could he really be comparing himself to the Passover Lamb? Could he really mean that he must give his body and his blood so that they could be spared?

Jesus looked up from the cup and passed his compassionate eyes over his disciples. He had been taken into their homes. He had dined with them. He had lived with them. They had loved him. But it was time for him to be taken out of the house, out of the city. It was time for him to be stricken down. It was time for his blood to be spilled and it would paint the wood of the cross. He looked over his disciples.

Eleven of them would partake of his life and his blood; they would find life in him. Peter would be a great teacher once he was restored. For even now, Jesus knew that Peter would soon deny knowing him. James would soon be put to death. John would write beautifully. He knew the time had come to die. Judas had left already and would find Jesus later in the garden praying, betraying him there to set in motion the events that would change the world. It was time to die (12)! Blood would be poured out for these men, and not only these, but for all who would be saved from the coming judgment of God.

Jesus would be the Passover Lamb. He was the Lamb who would take away the sin of the world (13). His blood would save mankind, but those who would not come under it, those who would not receive it, would face the wrath of God (14). God will come again to bring judgment on the earth, and those who have not partaken of the Passover Lamb that Jesus became will find themselves weeping and gnashing their teeth in an outcry that far exceeds that of the Egyptians (15).

The Passover! How richly it points us to the *one* who can save us. His blood and his body given so that God might pass over us in his wrath so we could be called the people of God, set free from sin, and taken over to the Promised Land prepared for us. See how the shadow of the Passover falls at the foot of the cross.

Glory to God!

Index of Scripture Chapter Six

1. Exodus Chapters 7–10 outline the first nine plagues that fell on Egypt including: water turned to blood, frogs, gnats, flies, death of cattle, boils, hail, locusts, and darkness.

2. Exodus 12:7, 12, 13 "Now the Lord said to Moses and Aaron in the land of Egypt, 'This month shall be the beginning of months for you; it is to be the first month of the year to you. Speak to all the congregation of Israel, saying, "On the tenth of this month they are each one to take a lamb for themselves, according to their households. Your lamb shall be unblemished. You shall keep it until the fourteenth day of the same month, then the whole assembly of the congregation of Israel is to kill it at twilight. Moreover, they shall take some of the blood and put it on the two doorposts and on the lintel of the houses in which they eat." For I will go through the land of Egypt on that night, and will strike down all the firstborn in the land of Egypt, both man and beast. The blood shall be a sign for you on the houses where you live; and when I see the blood I will pass over you, and no plague will befall you to destroy you when I strike the land of Egypt.'"

3. Exodus 12:35–36 "Now the sons of Israel had done according to the word of Moses, for they had requested from the Egyptians articles of

silver and articles of gold, and clothing; and the Lord had given the people favor in the sight of the Egyptians, so that they let them have their request. Therefore they plundered the Egyptians."

4. Exodus 12:8 "They shall eat the flesh that same night, roasted with fire, and they shall eat it with unleavened bread and bitter herbs."

5. Exodus 12:4 "Now if the household is too small for a lamb, then he and his neighbor nearest to his house are to take one according to what each man should eat, you are to divide the lamb."

6. Exodus 12: 29–30 "Now it came about at midnight that the Lord struck all the firstborn in the land of Egypt, from the firstborn of Pharaoh who sat on his throne to the firstborn of the captive who was in the dungeon, and all the firstborn of the cattle. Pharaoh arose in the night, he and all his servants and all the Egyptians, and there was a great cry in Egypt, for there was no home where there was not someone dead."

7. Exodus 11:6 "Moreover, there shall be a great cry in all the land of Egypt, such as there has not been before and such as shall never be again."

8. Exodus 12:33 "The Egyptians urged the people, to send them out of the land in haste, for they said, 'We will all be dead.'"

9. Matthew 14:25 "And in the fourth watch of the night [Jesus] came walking to them on the sea." Matthew 14: 19–21 "Jesus took the five loaves and the two fish, blessed the food, and breaking the loaves gave them to the disciples, and the disciples gave them to the crowds. There were about five thousand men who ate, besides women and children." Matthew 17:18 "Jesus rebuked him, and the demon came out, and the boy was cured at once." John 11: 43–44 "He cried out with a loud voice, 'Lazarus, come forth.' The man who had died came forth, bound hand and foot with wrappings, and his face was wrapped with a cloth."

10. Luke 22:19 "And when he had taken some bread and given thanks, he broke it and gave it to them, saying, 'This is my body which is given for you; do this in remembrance of me.'"

11. Luke 22: 20 "And in the same way he took the cup after they had eaten, saying, 'This cup which is poured out for you in the new covenant in my blood.'"

12. Luke 26: 72 "And again Peter denied it with an oath, 'I do not know the man.'" Acts 12:2 "And he had James the brother of John put to death with a sword." (John wrote the books of John, 1, 2, 3 John and Revelation.) Luke 22:47–48 "While he was speaking, a crowd came, and the one called Judas, one of the twelve, was with them; and he approached Jesus to kiss

him. But Jesus said to him, 'Judas, are you betraying the Son of Man with a kiss?'"

13. John 1:29 "The next day he saw Jesus coming to him and said, 'Behold, the Lamb of God who takes away the sin of the world!'"

14. John 3:36 "He who believes in the Son has eternal life; but he who does not obey the Son will not see life, but the wrath of God abides on him." Romans 5:9 "Having now been justified by his blood, we shall be saved from the wrath of God through him."

15. Matthew 13:41–42 "The Son of Man will send forth his angels, and they will gather out of his kingdom all the stumbling blocks, and those who commit lawlessness, and will throw them into the furnace of fire; in that place there will be weeping and gnashing of teeth."

EXODUS 15, 17:

The sweet tree and stricken Rock

The people fled from Egypt. These slaves were not yet accustomed to freedom. In fleeing, they became weary and burdened. Just days after having their shackles removed and the whip lifted from their sunburned shoulders, they found themselves following Moses through the desert. The dust had caked their dry lips. Each skin of water had been checked and rechecked to see if a drop of life lingered. But there was nothing. Three days in the wilderness and even the most resolute heart had become heavy (1).

But here was water! An oasis with green grass and the cool shadows of the trees! Tired feet ran with renewed energy and faces were thrust into the desert pool! Those who had come first drank deeply taking in great gulps of water. But the joy on each face and the sparkle in each eye would not last. The water had been swallowed rapidly, but oh how bitter it was! It turned the stomach and soured the tongue. "Don't drink it!" the cries echoed out around the pool. "It is bitter. It is not good for drinking"(2).

However, the thirsty were unhindered. Driven by cottony mouths, each in turn pushed forward, some drinking more timidly than others, but each finding the water bitter and unfit for refreshing a weary soul.

Resolute hearts had become heavy and now heavy hearts were filled with seething rage. The congregation turned to Moses and flagellated him with bitter tongues, "Moses, what are we supposed to drink now? Have you brought us out of slavery in Egypt to see us die in the desert?"(3)

Each violent cry battered the ears of Moses and he cried out to the LORD for help. Then came the voice, "Moses."

"Yes, LORD," Moses whispered.

"Moses, do you see that tree there?"

The servant lifted up his eyes and saw not many feet from him a small tree.

"Yes, LORD, I see it."

"Throw it into the waters and it will heal them and make them sweet" (4).

Moses rose from his knees and took hold of the tree. He grunted as he lifted it from the soil and heaved it into the bitter desert pool. Ripples fled away from the tree's violent interruption and raced to the shores, gently lapping at the mud and grasses.

Moses looked but nothing seemed to happen.

The water didn't spin or change colors. There was just the quieting of the ripples as they began to relax and calm themselves. The multitude looked to their leader whom they had just berated. Silence filled each mouth. Puzzled expressions filled each face. Moses met each face before his own with a solemn gaze and bent his face to the water. At first, he sipped.

Wait! Oh, it is sweet! He drank deeply of the cool water. It caressed his lips and moistened his tongue. He was so delighted at the refreshment that he forgot the crowds. He looked up to see the questioning many.

"It's sweet!" he said simply.

So they came to test the waters again. Bitter waters had been made sweet! The tree had taken that which was sour and made it life-giving. The tree had saved them! They would forget it soon enough, but for now it had made all the difference (5).

A few weeks passed and the people found themselves once again deep in the dryness of the desert. The hope in every chest was that the next hill crested would reveal a fresh stream that had been previously hidden. Every leaden step drug slowly forward. Miles had been traversed since the LORD had made the oasis waters sweet, and hearts began to reek of bitterness again. Quarreling erupted with sulfuric violence and shook the camp like an earthquake.

"Moses, this is entirely your fault! Give us water that we may drink! You have brought us up from Egypt, and for what? To kill us, our children, and our livestock with thirst?"(6).

The mob was ferocious in its attack, but Moses did as he always had done. Moses stopped where he stood and fell to his knees crying out with a loud voice, "LORD, what shall I do to this people? If you let this go on any longer they shall certainly put me to death" (7). Truly murder had already cast its dark color over the forehead of many who had gathered around. White knuckles had firm grips on staffs and stones just waiting to be bloodied.

"Moses, pass in front of the people with your staff in your hand and go over to the rock and strike it! Water will come out and will satisfy the craving of all who are thirsty" (8).

Moses cast a furtive glance at the weathered staff laying to the left of his face. Just a few weeks ago he had seen the same staff turn into a serpent. He had used this staff to turn the Nile into blood, and he had held it aloft and seen the Red Sea divided. His aged hand reached over for the staff and took hold of it. It felt smooth in his hands, and strong too! He pulled himself up from his knees to his full height and set his jaw, determined to do the work of God. Passing before the murderous crowd, Moses moved toward the rock.

Moses looked at those who would demand his life should their thirst not be quickly quenched. He took firm hold of the staff in two fists and with a warrior's cry swung it once over his head and brought it heavily upon the rock!

In an instant, the rock split apart and poured forth a river of water. This was no trickle but rather a current! Moses' feet were immediately bathed in the refreshing stream. The multitudes were divided as the torrent made its way across the desert floor, painting pale sand in dark and muddy hues. The animals took less pause than the people for the people were stunned. A gentle murmur of surprise and whispers of excitement made their way from those in view of the rock to those who were further back. They had been counted and were found to number 600,000 men, not counting women and children. There was water enough for them all.

None drank sparingly. The cool liquid dripped down into each belly and made each heart happy. The strong rock had been dealt a violent blow and from its wound poured forth a river of living water! The rock that had been struck had saved them (9).

Soon, however, they would forget the rock.

†

Jesus hung limp and heavy on the tree. He had been arrested about midnight and had been beaten. Many fists had pummeled and bruised his face. His eyes were swollen and were little more than slits on his crimson face. He had borne the tree, that wretched and glorious cross, to Golgotha. They had laid him on it and driven spikes into his hands and feet. The cross had been dropped into the hole prepared for it, and Jesus' body was rocked by the stop, his shoulders being pulled from their joints. The Savior's back in ragged strips painted the wood of the cross a scarlet shade. Thick red drops leapt from the piercing wounds of the thorny crown. He looked with blurry eyes over those gathered around him, each with murder in his heart. He knew they were perishing. He knew they were in drought and in famine, desperately in need of the water that brings life.

He had told them that he was God. Some had understood. He was the one who was going to give them living water (10). But they had despised him and the refreshment he had brought.

The wicked spewed forth curses with great force, and each one landed firmly in Jesus' heart.

But there were some who were beginning to understand.

There were some who saw the truth.

The cross, this twisted tree, would make sweet what once had been bitter. Where there had been a promise of death, this rugged tree would bring life. Where there was hopelessness, this tree would bring hope (11).

Not only that, but Christ the rock had been struck with great violence and from his wound had flowed life to all who would partake of it (12).

Take courage you who are thirsty in this life. Take courage you who feel that your hope has died. Boldly lift up your head, and see the tree that makes sweet the bitter waters. With weeping, look upon Christ, your rock, who was struck so that you might imbibe deeply of the river of delights.

The tree has saved you and the rock has imparted life!

Scripture Index for Chapter Seven

1. Exodus 15:22 "Moses led Israel from the Red Sea, and they went out into the wilderness of Shur; and they went three days in the wilderness and found no water."

2. Exodus 15:23 "When they came to Marah, they could not drink the waters of Marah, for they were bitter." Marah means "bitter."

3. Exodus 15:24 "So the people grumbled at Moses, saying, 'What shall we drink?'"

4. Exodus 15:25 "Then [Moses] cried out to the Lord, and the Lord showed him a tree; and he threw it into the waters."

5. Exodus 15: 25 "And the waters became sweet."

6. Exodus 17:2–3 "Therefore the people quarreled with Moses and said, 'Give us water that we may drink.' The people thirsted there for water; and they grumbled against Moses and said, 'Why, now, have you brought us up from Egypt, to kill us and our children and our livestock with thirst?'"

7. Exodus 17:4 "So Moses cried out to the Lord, saying, 'What shall I do to this people? A little more and they will stone me.'"

8. Exodus 17: 5–6 "Then the Lord said to Moses, 'Pass before the people and take with you some of the elders of Israel; and take in your hand your staff with which you struck the Nile, and

go. Behold, I will stand before you there on the rock at Horeb; and you shall strike the rock, and water will come out of it and the people may drink.' And Moses did so in the sight of the elders of Israel."

9. Psalm 78:15–17 "God split the rocks in the wilderness and gave them abundant drink like the ocean depths. He brought forth streams also from the rock and caused the waters to run down like rivers. Yet they continued to sin against him, to rebel against the Most High in the desert."

10. John 4:10 "If you knew the gift of God, you would have asked him, and he would have given you living water."

11. Colossians 2:13–14 "When you were dead in your sins, [God] made you alive together with [Christ], having forgiven us all our transgressions, having canceled out the certificate of debt consisting of decrees against us, which was hostile to us; and he has taken it out of the way, having nailed it to the cross."

12. 1 Corinthians 10:4 "They all drank the same spiritual drink, for they were drinking from a spiritual rock which followed them; and the rock was Christ."

EXODUS 16:

The Bread of Life, the Hidden Manna

The cool of the morning was already bustling with life. As the sun stretched itself from sleep and drew back the curtains of night, people emerged from their tents, baskets in hand. Not many days before, they had grumbled against Moses and the Holy God, outraged by their lack of food (1). Now every morning they rose when the cool wind of dawn stirs the desert flower gently waking it to behold the new day. When the shadows were long and painted in the purple of day-break, and the dew like many diamonds glistened on the ground, it was then that man, woman, and child departed from the warmth of their beds and came blinking into the soft rays.

God had given them food.

There, mingled with the dew was the bread that

had been rained down out of heaven. As the dew would evaporate in the dry desert air, fine flakes, frost-like in appearance, covered the earth (2). Then, as many purposeful ants set to a task, families would run about gathering much or little of this wafer. It was as sweet as honey in the mouth, and there was always enough so that each person should be made fully satisfied (3).

Yet there were a few provisions. This bread was only sufficient for the day at hand and those who found themselves blanketed in laziness would find that this manna, for so it was called, had melted away in the heat of the day (4). Furthermore, those who fearfully distrusted the provision of God and would horde great quantities of the angelic food to be kept for the following day would find it quite foul and unpalatable. For the simple fact was that manna did not last. It was perishable. Those who kept the bread in jars and pots with hopes that it would endure the night instead found it full of maggots and emitting a pungent odor (5).

So it went, day after day the people rose in the early hours to gather what food they could and make a meal of it, either boiling or baking it (6).

There were but two exceptions to the rapid decay of this manna. First of all, God had directed the people of Israel to do no work on the seventh day of the week. God in his wisdom and powerful provision allowed that the manna gathered on the sixth day should last for a full two days so that none would hunger on the Sabbath. Still some would foolishly exit their tents on the day of rest seeking for the miraculous biscuit and find that it was not there (7). Others would seek to keep the manna for a third day, supposing that it had different properties, but alas it too had become full of worms and stench. Even this manna eventually perished, having a life that lasted only a little longer than the manna gathered throughout the rest of the week.

The second exception to perishable manna was quite extraordinary. Just a few days after God had first rained manna upon the desert floor, he beckoned Moses to himself, "Moses, let an omerful of manna be kept in my presence throughout all of your generations. Put it in a golden jar and keep it in the ark of the covenant" (8).

Moses wasn't allowed to look upon the ark and certainly couldn't touch it, so he went to his brother Aaron, who was high priest at the time and relayed the command of God to him. Aaron on the next day gathered in a jar the manna that God had commanded to be kept in his presence forever and, having sealed the jar, placed it in the holy of holies.

The first day of the week, the people labored for their bread, and it was consumed; and if not consumed, became spoiled. So their labor continued. But the manna in God's presence remained fresh.

On the second day of the week, the people bent their backs to gather this bread, and they baked it and ate it, and that which was not eaten bred maggots. Their labor continued, but the manna in God's presence was sweet.

The third, fourth, and fifth days found people hurrying to gather food before the sun threatened to melt away their provision. They boiled it for dinner and that

which was not eaten stunk viciously. Their labor continued, but the manna in God's presence tasted of honey.

On the sixth day, a double portion was gathered
and endured just long enough to get through the seventh day, but whatever manna had been kept until the
first day of the week was found to be wriggling with
worms. So the people continued in their labor. For forty
years they bent their backs and hurried to gather food
to sustain their weary souls, but all of their labor failed
and none of that which they gathered ever endured.

But the manna in God's presence remained fresh
and sweet, tasting of honey, fragile and flakey. It was a
memorial forever of the saving power of God.

So the forty years passed in the desert, and the
manna ceased to come. The fruit of the Promised Land
had replaced the bread (9). Wars bathed the land and
judges ruled wisely. The people demanded a king. They
did get one, but he departed from the LORD and another
king was sought. His name was David and he loved the
LORD. His son Solomon became king, and during his
rule he built a grand and glorious temple for the LORD.
(It took seven and a half years.) In that temple was the
ark of the covenant, and in that ark was a golden jar
holding manna (10). Though manna had ceased to be
given more than 400 years before, and long after those
who had labored so hard for it had been laid to rest in
the earth, there was still the manna that God had commanded be put in his presence.

That manna had lasted.

That manna had remained.

When all that men could gather had rotted and
melted away, the hidden manna, kept by God, endured!

Men had tirelessly spent their energies only to find that all they had spent their sweat on had failed them again. Yet the manna in that golden jar that the High Priest had put aside would never fail!

†

Several thousand years passed and Jesus stood on a hillside. Multitudes had gathered around to hear him teach and preach. As they gathered around, Jesus spoke to Philip, "Where are we to buy bread, so that these may eat?"

Philip gaped with wide eyes, baffled that the Master would ask such a question, "Even with a year's wages we could not feed so many."

But Jesus already knew what he was going to do. A faint smile drew across his lips, "Have the people sit down and bring me the five loaves of bread and the two small fish" (11). The request seemed so strange. What could possibly be gained by so few pieces of food? How could so many be satisfied by such a pittance of bread? But the disciples did as the Master had said. Jesus stood and broke the bread and fish between the twelve that were following him, and with gentleness in his eyes said, "Take and give this to the people. Give as much as they want. When all are finished eating gather up what remains." So the disciples distributed food to the men, women, and children on the hillside, and all were fed abundantly. Furthermore twelve baskets full of food were left over (12).

What a fantastic miracle! Yet those who had been fed were slow to be impressed, and the following day

113

they came up to Jesus again wishing to be fed (13). Their selfish appetites kept them from seeing that Jesus was their Savior; they settled to have him as their waiter. As the crowd gathered again, Jesus spoke resolutely, "You seek me, because you ate the loaves and were filled. But do not work for the food which perishes, but for the food which endures to eternal life."

"Impress us!" The voices were shouting. "Do some sign or some work, and we will believe you! Our ancestors ate manna in the wilderness. Bread out of heaven was given to them. Do that for us, and we will believe that you are the Savior" (14).

Jesus looked over them with compassion and sorrow, "I am the bread of life," he said. "Come to me, and you will not hunger. I am the bread that comes down from heaven. Your fathers ate the manna in the wilderness and died. But I am the living bread, I am the true manna, he who eats of me will never die" (15).

The rabble became indignant arguing with one another. They were followers of the Law. They worked hard for righteousness and holiness, and now this one dared to tell them that life, real and powerful, could be found in him alone! The words of Christ stung their arrogant hearts.

"How dare he tell us not to work for food that perishes! How dare he tell us that he is the bread of life! How dare he speak to us in this manner!" Each one began to hold high his credentials like a banner.

"I'm a teacher of the Law."

"I faithfully attend the synagogue."

"I give to the poor."

"I have touched the sick and diseased."

"I am a good husband."

"I am a compassionate mother."

Little did they know that all they had labored for would perish. Little did they understand that those things they called life-giving would not last. Every day they would sweat and hurry and bend their backs to do work. Every day they would lay their heads on their beds believing that they had stored up enough holiness or righteousness to last until tomorrow. Yet every morning they would wake to find that all they had broken their backs for the previous day had rotted and was full of death, bearing the stench of the grave. They didn't comprehend that it was not their labor that would last, and it made hot their blood and stung their hearts to think that real life could be found only in this one called Jesus.

So enraged with stubborn hearts and flinty heads they departed from the one who could save them and returned to their tiresome labor hoping that today's work would be sufficient to please the living God (16). And they, like their forefathers, died.

But some, a small handful of men, stayed behind. The voice of Jesus broke the silence as the dust of the departed settled, "You do not want to go away too, do you?"

Peter looked around at those who remained, "LORD, where would we go? You have the words of eternal life" (17).

Sinner, learn the lesson of the manna. It is not what you can do that will save you. It is not what you labor for that lasts. All of your work will fail. All of your labor will result in death alone. All of your church attendance and good deeds will not save you. But there is a High Priest modeled after Aaron, and he has given his body as manna that is kept forever in the presence of God. Cease your striving, and come under the yoke borne on the back of Jesus and find that his strength is sufficient to save. Find that his labor and not yours will provide rest for your soul (18). He is the bread of life. He cannot perish. He cannot be destroyed. His name is Jesus. Be certain that he called himself "manna", but he is not the kind of manna for which we sweat. He is not the manna that melts away in the heat of trouble. He is not the manna that breeds a foul odor or death if kept too long. He is the manna that endures! He is forever in the presence of his Father as a memorial of the life he alone can give. Partake of Christ! Partake of this hidden manna! Rest your weary shoulders. Those who will not cease all their strivings will certainly face a hellish death. But to those who overcome and take hold of Christ in this world, they will partake of him, the hidden manna, in heaven forever (19). Take note of that. Look at it again. The promise for those who overcome this world and cross the threshold into heaven is that we get to partake of the hidden manna. We get to partake of that which lasts forever. To be certain we have partaken of Christ now as believers bathed in his blood, but we have not fully partaken of him. On the other side of the grave we will have the presence of the LORD opened before us and there will be our life-giving bread, and we will call his name "Jesus."

Scripture Index for Chapter Eight

1. Exodus 16: 2–3 "The whole congregation of the sons of Israel grumbled against Moses and Aaron in the wilderness. The sons of Israel said to them, 'Would that we had died by the Lord's hand in the land of Egypt, when we sat by the pots of meat, when we ate bread to the full; for you have brought us out into this wilderness to kill this whole assembly with hunger.'"

2. Exodus 16:13–14 "So it came about at evening that the quails came up and covered the camp, and in the morning there was a layer of dew around the camp. When the layer of dew evaporated, behold, on the surface of the wilderness there was a fine flake-like thing, fine as the frost on the ground."

3. Exodus 16: 17–18, 31 "The sons of Israel gathered much and some gathered little. When they measured it with an omer, he who had gathered much had no excess, and he who gathered little had no lack; every man gathered as much as he should eat. The house of Israel named it manna, and it was like coriander seed, white, and its taste was like wafers with honey." [Author Note: "Manna" literally means, "what is it." The people called it "what is it" for forty years.]

4. Exodus 16:21 "They gathered it morning by morning, every man as much as he should eat; but when the sun grew hot, it would melt."

5. Exodus 16:20 "But they did not listen to Moses, and some left part of it until morning, and it bred maggots and became foul; and Moses was angry with them."

6. Exodus 16:23 "Bake what you will bake and boil what you will boil."

7. Exodus 16:27 "It came about on the seventh day [Sabbath] that some of the people went out to gather, but they found none."

8. Exodus 16:32–33 "Then Moses said, 'This is what the Lord has commanded, "Let an omerful of it be kept throughout your generations, that they may see the bread that I fed you in the wilderness, when I brought you out of Egypt."' Moses said to Aaron, 'Take a jar and put an omerful of manna in it, and place it before the Lord to be kept throughout your generations.'"

9. Joshua 5:11–12 "On the day after the Passover, on that very day, they ate some of the produce of the land, unleavened cakes and parched grain. The manna ceased on the day after they had eaten some of the produce of the land, so that the sons of Israel no longer had manna, but they ate some of the yield of the land of Canaan during that year."

10. Hebrews 9:4 "The ark of the covenant was covered on all sides with gold, in which was a golden jar holding manna, and Aaron's rod that budded, and the tablets of the covenant."

11. John 6:5–11 "Jesus, lifting up his eyes and seeing that a large crowd was coming to him, said to Philip, 'Where are we going to buy bread, so that these may eat?' This he was saying to test him, for he himself knew what he was intending to do. Philip answered, 'Two hundred denarii worth of bread is not sufficient for them.' Jesus said, 'Have the people sit down.' Jesus then took the loaves, and having given thanks, he distributed to those who were seated; likewise also of the fish as much as they wanted."

12. John 6:12–13 "When they were filled, Jesus said to his disciples, 'Gather up the leftover fragments so that nothing will be lost.' So they gathered them up and filled twelve baskets with fragments."

13. John 6:26 "Jesus answered them and said, 'Truly, truly, I say to you, you are seeking me, not because you saw miracles, but because you ate the loaves and were filled.'"

14. John 6:30–31 "So they said to him, 'What then do you do for a sign, so that we may see, and believe you? What work do you perform? Our fathers ate the manna in the wilderness; as it is written, "He gave them bread out of heaven to eat."'"

15. John 6:35, 41–42, 48–51, 54–58 "Jesus said to them, 'I am the bread of life; he who comes to me will not hunger, and he who believes in me will not thirst. I am the bread that came down out of heaven. I have come down out of heaven. I am the bread of life. Your fathers ate the manna in the wilderness, and they died. This is the bread, which comes down out of heaven, so that one may eat of it and not die. I am the living bread that came down out of heaven; if anyone eats of this bread, he will live forever; and the bread also which I give for the life of the world is my flesh. For my flesh is true food, and my blood is true drink. As the living Father sent me, and I live because of the Father, so he who eats me, he also will live because of me. This is the bread which came down out of heaven; not as the fathers ate and died; he who eats this bread will live forever.'"

16. John 6:61, 66 "Therefore many of his disciples, when they heard this said, 'This is a difficult statement; who can listen to it?' As a result of this many of his disciples withdrew and were not walking with him anymore."

17. John 6:67–68 "So Jesus said to the twelve, 'You do not want to go away also, do you?' Simon Peter answered him, 'Lord, to whom shall we go? You have the words of eternal life.'"

18. Matthew 11:28–30 "Come to me, all who are weary and heavy-laden, and I will give you rest. Take my yoke upon you and learn from

me, for I am gentle and humble in heart, and you will find rest for your souls. For my yoke is easy and my burden is light."

19. Revelation 2:17 "He who has an ear, let him hear what the Spirit says to him who overcomes, to him I will give some of the hidden manna, and I will give him a white stone, and a new name written on the stone which no one knows but he who receives it."

NUMBERS 21:

The Lifting up of the One who Saves Us

The sun seemed to be thrust into blackness as night forcefully came upon the camp of the Hebrews. An eerie calm rested on the tents where just moments before venomous cursing had been poured forth from lips and throats, open like graves. The whole of the multitude had risen up against Moses and the God who had thus far preserved them in the land. Though they had been amply fed with the bread of angels and though the rock had been split now a second time to bring out rivers of refreshing, the people complained for lack of food and drink (1). Though God had been gracious to sustain them almost forty years without a need for fresh sandals or a new shirt, weariness and discontentment swept over them like a flood and buried their hearts in rage (2). Their complaint was no different than it had been when all those years before they had left the slavery of Egypt.

"Why have you brought us out of Egypt to see us die in this desert?" The poisonous words dripped from their tongues. They accused the gracious God of heaven. They blasphemed and spewed forth the bile of resentment (3).

But now the curses had been put to bed. The fury had caused each tired heart to fail and the crowd dispersed.

The calm was almost a person itself. It was so quiet and towered like a giant over the camp. It was a secret enemy coming to smite the wicked. And that is exactly what it was. The cries of the wicked had risen to heaven, and the God of all creation was moved, not to save or to intervene but to destroy.

Had we seen the wrath of God pour out from heaven that night, our knees would have been too feeble to hold us, and our countenance would have been painted in deathly hues. But to the wicked heart there is no concern of wrath or judgment. So even as they lay in bed, their violent oaths whispered them to sleep and those who had clothed themselves with curses now found it entering their bodies like water and oil in their bones (4).

There was one whose heart was uneasy. Moses had fallen to his face as the curses fell upon his head like many blows. His tears had been poured out before the LORD like a pleasing drink offering. Moses had been here before. He knew the flame of God's wrath had been kindled and his bowels quaked within him. He knew that the great enemy called death had come into the camp and that none should be saved unless God could be moved.

A gentle rustling alone disturbed the silence. The sound was like the reeds that rustle in the gentle current of the stream or perhaps when one grinds slowly the grain with the stone. At first there would be no reason for an ear to perceive it, but this was not the sound of a casual bubbling brook or one who was grinding grain for a simple loaf. It seemed that the rustling or scraping, as it was, came from every direction and every part of the camp.

The terror grew in each heart as the advancing army drew nearer. Sleepers were roused from dreams as the assassins closed in. Some of the wicked would cast a light into the dark shadow of the room just in time to see the deadly assailant lunge forward. Others sat in darkness hoping that whatever it was that waited would pass them by.

Each fiery serpent looked with black eyes lustfully over those they had been sent to strike. In dark or light each raced forward to their prey. Seen or unseen each pointed tooth dripped with anticipation.

Then in that lightning flash of a moment when they struck and hid their fangs in the flesh of man, in that instant when their venom pumped through veins, they would have been apparent! The blinding pain of a burning coal would have swept through the body of each who had been so violently accosted. Cold sweat would have broken out on each brow as a lamp was lit and a wound examined; and there in the corner or there in the fold of a blanket would have been the culprit, that wicked serpent bent on killing.

There wouldn't be one among the camp who was safe. Child and adult alike would fall victim to the poison. With a tightening chest, fingers curled about in agony, and lips drawn thin and tense, the color would drain from each face, and without fail the heart would slow and finally stop.

The serpents had come to kill and they had done their job well (5).

The night that earlier had been full of angry voices was now full of fear as terror cast its shadow through every tent. Screams of agony were being raised to heaven as the people ground their teeth together from the pain.

In haste the people made their way to Moses with prayers of repentance on their lips, "We have sinned, because we have spoken against the LORD and you. Intercede with the LORD, that he may remove the serpents from us" (6).

And Moses did, but the LORD would not take the serpents away. He would not keep them from biting. The poison would still course through the veins of the afflicted. Still the LORD did provide a balm. God looked on the dying with mercy and constructed a way that they might be saved.

"Moses, make a fiery serpent out of bronze, and put it on a pole; it shall come about, that everyone who is bitten, when he looks at it, he will live" (7). The instructions seemed easy enough. Moses hurried to heat the bronze. He labored with the hammer and the chisel and fashioned a great snake. He set it on a high pole so that it could be seen throughout the camp. With help he raised the pole, set it in place, and then stood before the congregation.

"When any of you find yourself bitten by the serpent and your life in peril because of its venom, look here to the bronze serpent raised up in your midst and you shall live." Some mocked and some ridiculed. Pride would keep some from looking and they would pay with their lives. Disbelief kept others from raising up their eyes. Yet many, when bitten, were quick to run to the pole and gaze upon the serpent; and all who looked upon it lived. They still bore on their body the mark where the fangs had pierced their flesh. Undoubtedly the venom still coursed through their bodies, but the miracle was that the venom now held no power over them. They had been rescued from the plague that befell them.

†

Jesus' bloody body hung from the cross in tatters. The wood beneath his body was adorned in the most garish hue. His swollen eyes looked over those who had gathered around him to mock and to curse. Their eyes had been blinded and their hearts so hardened they could not see it or perceive it, but he could see that the ancient serpent called Satan had crept in unnoticed. That vile enemy of all mankind had struck, and he had infected all with the poison of sin (8).

Jesus blinked the blood away to look upon them again. They were dying. They were raging against God and all those who had spoken for him. They were infected. Sin was coursing through their bodies of flesh and dust and they had no idea that it would kill them.

But there were a few who felt the poison of their sin. There were those who had stood before the living God and had repented and cried out for his saving hand. He had fashioned a Savior for them. He had set him on a pole in the midst of the congregation and had bid them to look on the One who had been raised up on their behalf.

There was a man among those gathered at the bloody feet of Jesus. He did not mock nor did he curse. He was waiting. He had come to bury this Savior of men. He had come to anoint the broken body of his LORD. The dying one, the one raised up, was breathing his last and Nicodemus began to weep (9). He knew what was happening here. He had read the Scripture. He knew about the serpent in the wilderness. When Jesus had been ministering, Nicodemus used to come to him by night for instruction, and now as he stood on the fringe, he called to mind the words of this Christ: "As Moses lifted up the serpent in the wilderness, even so must the Son of Man be lifted up so that whoever believes will in him have eternal life" (10).

Nicodemus wept. The tears overwhelmed him like a tempest. His body shook with grief. He wanted to shout to the cursing crowd: "You've been bitten by the serpent of old! His venom now is in your heart! Death is all that you can hope for. Look upon the dying one.

See the one who has been raised up! Look to the one who can save you!"

But he was silent. He had tried to speak out before but had been criticized (11). Still as he looked upon the Savior his heart was comforted. The plague of sin and the power of the poison had been removed from him. It was true that the wound of sin was still upon his body and that the venom of sin still lived within him, but now its penalty and power had been destroyed.

Oh, sinner, don't you know that the poison of sin is in your heart and that it will certainly kill you? There is no escaping it on your own. But one was lifted up on your behalf, and he bids you look on him and believe. In Christ you will find your life. In Jesus your hope is found. Do not let pride or disbelief keep you from repentance. Hurry to the cross and gaze upon the one who saves! His name is Jesus!

Scripture Index for Chapter Nine

1. Psalm 78: 20, 24–25 "He struck the rock so that waters gushed out, and streams were overflowing; can he give bread also? He rained down manna upon them to eat and gave them food from heaven. Man did eat the bread of angels; he sent them food in abundance."

2. Deuteronomy 8:4 "Your clothing did not wear out on you, nor did your food swell these forty years."

3. Numbers 21:5 "The people spoke against God and Moses, 'Why have you brought us up out of Egypt to die in the wilderness? For there is no food and no water, and we loathe this miserable food.'"

4. Psalm 109:18 "But he clothed himself with cursing as with his garment, and it entered into his body like water and like oil into his bones."

5. Numbers 21: 6 "The Lord sent fiery serpents among the people and they bit the people, so that many people of Israel died."

6. Numbers 21:7 "So the people came to Moses and said, 'We have sinned, because we have spoken against the Lord and you; intercede with the Lord, that he may remove the serpents from us.' And Moses interceded for the people."

7. Numbers 21:8 "Then the Lord said to Moses, 'Make a fiery serpent, and set it on a standard;

and it shall come about, that everyone who is bitten, when he looks at it, he will live.'"

8. Revelation 12:9 "And the great dragon was thrown down, the serpent of old who is called the devil and Satan, who deceives the whole world; he was thrown down to the earth, and his angels were thrown down with him." Revelation 20:2 "And he laid hold of the dragon, the serpent of old, who is the devil and Satan, and bound him for a thousand years."

9. John 19:38–39 "Joseph of Arimathea asked Pilate that he might take away the body of Jesus; and Pilate granted permission. So he came and took away his body. Nicodemus, who had first come to [Jesus] by night, also came, bringing a mixture of myrrh and aloes, about a hundred pounds weight."

10. John 3:14–16 "As Moses lifted up the serpent in the wilderness, even so must the Son of Man be lifted up; so that whoever believes will in him have eternal life. For God so loved the world that he gave his only begotten Son, that whoever believes in him shall not perish, but have eternal life."

11. John 7:50–52 "Nicodemus (he who came to [Jesus] before, being one of them) said to them, 'Our Law does not judge a man unless it first hears from him and knows what he is doing, does it?' They answered him, 'You are not also from Galilee, are you? Search and see that no prophet arises out of Galilee.'"

DEUTERONOMY 21:

The One Who Bore the Curse of God

The scene was a surreal one and had it been viewed from a distance it would have seemed more like theater than real life. Joshua had led his army in battle and had, by the power of God, brought about a great victory. Five kings had been captured in the great raucous and had been locked away in a cave behind a great stone until Joshua could return from the battlefront.

But he was back. The dirt that covered his face was streaked with sweat and blood. Hand-to-hand combat could be fierce. His chest rose hard with each tired breath, and he stood powerfully before those who had followed him into battle. Joshua had fire in his eyes as he said to the chiefs of war that stood by his side, "Put your feet on the necks of these kings!" (1).

The five kings were thrust into the dirt and the men of war came and each laid a foot on the necks of the kings who had set themselves up against God and his holy people.

"Now do not fear or be dismayed," Joshua shouted to the crowds. "Be strong and courageous, for thus shall the LORD do to all of your enemies whom are at war with you" (2).

With that, Joshua took hold of his blood-soaked sword and with violent precision struck each of the five kings a deathblow (3).

"Hang each of them on a tree, and leave them there until sunset! Let them bear the full curse of God. For we know, according to the word of God, anyone who is hung on a tree is God's cursed one!" (4).

But on this day, the king's bodies were hoisted onto trees. This was to be done to anyone deserving death. This high and lofty shame would be heaped upon them. God had said they should not stay up all night, so that evening the corpses were pulled down from the trees and thrown into a hollow place in the rock. A large stone was rolled against the opening and those who had been cursed by the LORD God were laid down in silence. And they are there to this very day (5).

†

The scene was a surreal one and had it been viewed from a distance it would have seemed more like theater than real life. The Roman soldiers took the bloodied body of Christ Jesus and nailed it to the cross, that violent tree of death. They raised the wooden beam into the air and let it drop into the hole that had been prepared for it. You would think from the great tumult at the feet of Jesus that he had been taken in war as a prisoner. Now his executioners had hung him up for all to see.

The Savior hung on this tree, suffering the full measure of God's curse. A shadow of deep darkness blanketed the sky and turned noon to night (6). Unlike the kings of old that Joshua had hung up, it was not for his own wrongdoings that the Christ suffered so. Jesus had known that we weak and wicked people of the earth were under the wrath of God. He knew that we were, for all of our iniquity, deserving of the title "God's cursed one" (7).

But love compelled him (8).

Hanging there for our sins and not his own, Jesus suffered and died. He had become the curse for us so that we could be set free from the curse (9).

Just like those kings that Joshua hung up were removed before the setting sun, so also Jesus was taken down before the evening set upon his body. Christ was also laid in a cave. A stone was laid against the opening, and those who had viewed these happenings were silenced (10). But unlike those dead kings who remain buried in that cave to this day, our king shook the earth three days later and rose to life, for he is victorious over death in that it could not hold him. (11).

If you still find yourself denying God, if you still find yourself fighting against him then take warning!

The wrath of God remains on you, and you shall fall under his curse. You shall be cast away from him and find your eternity spent apart from him in hell. If you would be free from God's violent fury, if you would be called blessed rather than cursed, then hasten to take hold of him who was hung on the tree in your place. Call on your king who became your curse so that you could receive the promise of the spirit of God, which comes through faith. If you are reading these words, there is yet time for you to be set free from the curse of the tree!

Scripture Index for Chapter Ten

1. Joshua 10:24 "When they brought these kings out to Joshua, Joshua called for all the men of Israel, and said to the chiefs of the men of war who had gone with him, 'Come near, put your feet on the necks of these kings.' So they came near and put their feet on their necks."

2. Joshua 10:25 "Joshua then said to them, 'Do not fear or be dismayed! Be strong and courageous, for thus the Lord will do to all of your enemies with whom you fight.'"

3. Joshua 10:26 "So afterward Joshua struck them and put them to death, and he hanged them on five trees; and they hung on the trees until evening."

4. Deuteronomy 21:22, 23 "If a man has committed a sin worthy of death and he is put to death, and you hang him on a tree, his corpse shall not hang all night on the tree, but you shall surely bury him on the same day (for he who is hanged on the tree is accursed of God), so that you do not defile your land which the Lord your God gives you as an inheritance."

5. Joshua 10:27 "It came about at sunset that Joshua gave a command, and they took them down from the trees and threw them into the cave where they had hidden themselves, and put large stones over the mouth of the cave, to this very day."

6. Matthew 27:45 "Now from the sixth hour darkness fell upon all the land until the ninth hour."

7. John 3:36 "He who believes in the Son has eternal life; but he who does not obey the Son will not see life, but the wrath of God abides on him." Romans 2:5 "But because of your stubbornness and unrepentant heart you are storing up wrath for yourself in the day of wrath and revelation of the righteous judgment of God."

8. Romans 5:8 "But God demonstrates his own love toward us, in that while we were yet sinners, Christ died for us."

9. Galatians 3:13–14 "Christ redeemed us from the curse of the Law, having become a curse for us—for it is written, 'Cursed is everyone who hangs on a tree'—in order that in Christ Jesus the blessing of Abraham might come to the Gentiles, so that we would receive the promise of the Spirit through faith."

10. Matthew 27:57–61 "When it was evening, there came a rich man from Arimathea, named Joseph, who himself had also become a disciple of Jesus. This man went to Pilate and asked for the body of Jesus. Then Pilate ordered it to be given to him. And Joseph took the body and wrapped it in a clean linen cloth, and laid it in his own new tomb, which he had hewn out in the rock; and he rolled a large

stone against the entrance of the tomb and went away. Mary Magdalene was there, and the other Mary, sitting opposite the grave."

11. 1 Corinthians 15:3–4, 54–57 "Christ died for our sins according to the Scriptures, and he was buried, and he was raised on the third day according to the Scriptures. When the perishable will have put on the imperishable, and this mortal will have put on immortality, then will come about the saying that is written, 'Death is swallowed up in victory. O death, where is your victory? O death, where is your sting?' The sting of death is sin and the power of sin is the law; but thanks be to God, who gives us the victory through our Lord Jesus Christ."

JOSHUA 2:

Redeemed from the Coming Judgment

She sat across from the two men and watched in silence as they ate her bread and drank her water. She wasn't surprised by anything they had said, and it wasn't fear she was feeling now. Her mother had told her stories when she was a girl about how God had destroyed the Egyptians by his mighty power and how he was going to bring his people to the Promised Land. She knew, as all the citizens of Jericho did, this land that they had called home wasn't going to be theirs much longer. This land was to be the Promised Land of the Hebrews. She knew that she and all her people would be destroyed. These two men were just the forerunners. These were just the spies. There was an army waiting just beyond the river. Jericho would be their first stop, and they would leave it devastated.

She should have been afraid, but the trembling she felt wasn't from terror. She unconsciously played with the ends of her braids. The uneasiness in her stomach would not be quieted. There was no reason she should be embarrassed or ashamed, and yet it stung her cheeks like the blow of many fists.

Rahab looked back at the two who were finishing their meals. These men seemed so different than the others who had come to her home. These were somehow more dignified. They were soldiers to be sure. They carried themselves straight and came into her home without furtive glances over their shoulders. The others weren't interested in bread or water. The others were harsh.

Daily she would lie under the foul breath of sweaty men and let them have their way with her for pay. A coin would be tossed coldly on the table as the men would go one after the other. She had come to hate that sound. Every coin that rattled on the table or rung in her purse was a reminder of who she was and what it was she did for a living.

She hoped these two men wouldn't guess her profession but there was no denying it. Her eyes were painted heavily and her cheeks were red more from the blush than the ever-mounting shame. Her hair was braided with colorful cloth to show off the curves of her neck and shoulders. Her wrists and ankles were heavy with gold bracelets. Everything about her was an indicator of her line of work. Maybe that is why they would scarcely look in her direction. She pulled the shawl she was wearing a bit more tightly around her, trying desperately to demonstrate the modesty she had forgotten more than ten years ago.

"I know the LORD has given you this land." The sound of her own voice startled her. The spies looked up to see if she would continue. Rahab braced herself as she continued.

"Your terror has fallen upon us, and all the people of the land have melted away before you. We know how your God dried up the Red Sea before you when you left Egypt those many years ago, and we know what you have done to the kings beyond the Jordan, how you have utterly destroyed them. The very telling of it has caused all of our hearts to melt within us. These were the stories we were told as children. I know that your God is the LORD and he lives in heaven above and on the earth below. I know this land will be yours. Your God will give it to you" (1).

The men looked at each other wondering if they had been betrayed.

The sudden sound of heavy footsteps in the street put thoughts of betrayal firmly in their minds when soldiers were heard outside.

They had been discovered!

News of the spies had reached the king, and a search from door-to-door was ordered (2). The search party could be heard yelling and throwing things about in their efforts. These hearts did not seem to have melted with fear. Before a cry of surprise could be uttered, Rahab had grabbed the men by their hands and pulled them from the table. She didn't say a word as she led them up the stairs in the back of the house and out on to the roof. She lay the men down and signaled for them to be quiet as she covered them with stalks of flax (3). Then she stole quickly and quietly back into the house and removed the men's plates from the table. A moment later the soldiers were upon her, flooding the room. There were no formalities in the home of a prostitute, and they ransacked the place. She felt the heat of shame rising in her chest as she looked from face to face and realized that she knew most of them. Today they would terrorize her by devastating her home and tomorrow they would terrorize her body for a copper coin. The tears stung her eyes as she fought to hold them back. A gruff man who had kissed her face just this week grabbed her hard by the arm.

"Bring out the men who have come to you tonight. We know that they have come to spy on our land." His demanding nature was something to which she was accustomed.

Breathing deeply she found her voice more sure than she had expected, "Yes men came to me, but when it began to get dark they went out. I'm sure if you leave quickly you can still overtake them" (4).

The soldier shoved her hard against the wall and spat on her as he left, laughing about how the whore couldn't keep men in her home for very long and without another word they turned to leave.

Rahab fell into a heap on the floor and let the warm tears wash her cheeks. The sobs came heavy upon her and her body shook. If only the tears could wash away her pain, she thought to herself as she lay there in the dark.

When the streets grew quiet again she went to the roof to retrieve the spies and brought them back into her home. One of the men lit a small lamp and set it on the lamp stand to give light to the whole house while the other sat Rahab at the table and poured her some wine.

"We need to thank you," he spoke softly. It was the softness in his voice that gave her the courage to speak again.

"Swear to me that since I have been kind to you, that you will also be kind to me. When you come and the LORD God gives you this city, deliver my life from death. Along with my life, I ask for the life of my parents, my brothers and sisters, and all that they have with them" (5).

Her heart fell within her in that moment before they spoke. Her own words had sounded so foolish to her. She was a prostitute. Her own family only used her for the money she made. Why would these men spare her? If only she had been more noble or perhaps less boorish. She tried to rub the makeup from her cheeks with the back of her hand and sat up a bit straighter hoping they would look past her filth.

Their words came more quickly than she thought.

"Our soul for yours" (6).

Rahab wept.

The next few moments passed hurriedly. Rahab had gone out into the dark night and had returned with a length of rope. Making sure it was fastened firmly to the window she begged the men to climb down from the city wall and to make their escape.

"Please, go and hide in the hill country until the

search party has returned. They will look for you for three days. When they are done, you can go back to your army and bring them here. But remember your oath when you return," she almost found herself begging (7).

"Thank you for hiding us. We will return in a number of days." The spies traded glances once again before continuing, "We will be free from the oath we have made to you, unless, when we come into the land, you tie this cord of scarlet thread in the window. And be sure that all whom you would have us spare are gathered to you in this house. Should we come to this city and the scarlet cord not be in the window or your family not be gathered to your house, your blood will be on your own head." He took from his bag several feet of scarlet cord and pushed it into Rahab's hand. "Only this shall save you when we come" (8).

She trembled as she held the soft rope in her hand. To think that this simple piece of string should save her life.

"I'll do it just as you have said."

With that the men departed down the rope and into the inky shadow of night. Rahab had told them to wait for three days, but she knew that their army was ready and, being fearful that they may come back with the daylight, quickly tied the scarlet cord in the window. Then taking up her lamp she ran into the street to rouse her family in their beds and beg them to come to the house of the prostitute so that they may be saved when judgment came.

Between ten and fourteen days later, the army of the people of God showed up at Jericho. Joshua was leading them. He had been the leader of the people since Moses had died. This was the mighty Joshua. A man in whom dwelt the spirit of God. Rahab had wondered what had taken them so long. She had wondered if the spies had been caught, but whatever fear or doubt crept into her mind, she would not let her family leave and she would not remove the cord. Men had been turned away from the prostitute's home. She was going to have a new life now.

The conquest of Jericho took seven days, and on that seventh day the two who had dined with Rahab came to her and took her and all who were with her safely away. The rest of all that lived and breathed in Jericho were completely destroyed. Only those in the household of the scarlet cord were saved (9).

Rahab came into the Hebrew camp. She felt dirty among these "People of God." For the first few days, she hung her head low. She was, however, received graciously and given a tent for her and her household. She was given provisions and a few small sheep to care for. Soon she noticed that there seemed to be smiles on the faces of the Hebrews, and she began to lift her gaze to meet theirs more often. One day she caught a man staring intently at her, and she felt the flood of shame rising up again in her heart. But he smiled at her, spoke tenderly to her, and beckoned her to follow him. He loved her deeply, and she finally experienced love for the first time. Soon they were married. The two of them had a son named Boaz. Boaz would marry a foreign woman (maybe because his mother had been one) named Ruth, and they would have a son named Obed. Obed would have a son named Jesse, and Jesse would have a son David. This David would be king of all Israel and would point the way to the Messiah (10).

She who was a prostitute would be saved by the scarlet cord and become the great, great grandmother of Israel's greatest king. More than that, her name would be mentioned in the lineage of the Savior of mankind, the God-man Jesus!

†

We cannot help but see the great parallels between this fantastic text and the truths about our returning Savior, Jesus Christ. Joshua sits on the edge of the Jordan preparing to come and bring God's judgment on Jericho, and Jesus sits on the edge of heaven waiting for that moment that he would come and bring his judgment to a fallen world. His name means "Jehovah is Salvation" as did Joshua's name. Joshua sent in two men to spy out the land and we know that Jesus will send his two witnesses before him and so mark his eminent coming (11). Joshua brought the army of God with him, and when Jesus comes so shall his army come right at his heels (12). He is coming with a sword to strike down the nations and a rod of iron to rule them (13).

We do not know what day it will be when he steps from heaven to once again place his foot upon the earth (14) for he shall come like a thief in the night (15). But in this we have great confidence: Jesus will certainly spare those who are under the covering of his scarlet blood, those whose lives have been changed. It makes no difference what great and wicked sinners we were, if we should but tie the scarlet cord in the window, if we should come under the scarlet blood of Jesus we find that all is forgiven us! We will find that not only has the blood allowed for our forgiveness, but it has also changed our hearts and turned our eyes from sin to look upon the beautiful Savior. "Jehovah is Salvation" will come and rescue us instead of bringing destruction. He will call us his own people and welcome us in his tents. His blood that was spilled for us at Calvary is all that is able to save us. When he comes with his armies and sees the sign of his blood over us, as Joshua's men saw the scarlet cord, it shall be salvation for us and not destruction. Life and not death. Peace and not fear.

While we wait for that return, while we wait for "Jehovah our Salvation," let us lay aside our former wickedness and let us hurry to the streets and bring in all that we can to the household of the scarlet cord. Let us, as Rahab must have, feel a sense of urgency to find those around us and bring them under the scarlet blood of Jesus so that they too can be saved at his coming. Let us tell them of sin and judgment, of hope and life. Let us tell them of the simplicity of the blood of Jesus, which will be a covering for us. Let us gather as many as we can together, so that together we can be saved.

What a great and mighty salvation it shall be! For as Rahab was ushered into the tents of God's people and was married, so shall we—the church, the redeemed, the saved—be married to Christ Jesus, and we shall forever be listed in the lineage of the Savior of mankind, the God-man, Jesus!

Scripture Index for Chapter Eleven

1. Joshua 2:9–11 "I know that the LORD has given you the land, and that the terror of you has fallen on us, and that all the inhabitants of the land have melted away before you. We have heard how the LORD dried up the water of the Red Sea before you when you came out of Egypt, and what you did to the two kings beyond the Jordan. When we heard it, our hearts melted and no courage remained in any man any longer because of you; for the LORD your God, he is God in heaven above and on the earth beneath."

2. Joshua 2:3 "And the king of Jericho sent word to Rahab, saying, 'Bring out the men who have come to you, who have entered your house, for they have come to search out all the land.'"

3. Joshua 2:6 "But she had brought them up to the roof and hidden them in the stalks of flax which she had laid in order on the roof."

4. Joshua 2: 15–16 "Then she let them down by a rope through the window, for her house was on the city wall, so that she was living on the wall. She said to them, 'Go to the hill country, so that the pursuers will not happen upon you,

and hide yourselves there for three days. Then afterward you may go on your way.'"

5. Joshua 2:12–13 "Now therefore, please swear to me by the LORD, since I have dealt kindly with you, that you also will deal kindly with my father's household, and give me a pledge of truth, and spare my father and my mother and my brothers and my sisters, and all who belong to them, and deliver our lives from death."

6. Joshua 2:14 "So the men said to her, 'Our soul for yours if you do not tell this business of ours.'"

7. Joshua 2:16 "Hide yourselves for three days until the pursuers return."

8. Joshua 2:17–19 "We shall be free from this oath to you unless, when we come into the land, you tie this cord of scarlet in the window through which you let us down. Gather all the members of your household. It shall come about that anyone who leaves the doors of your house and goes into the street, his blood shall be on his own head."

9. Joshua 6: 23 "So the young men who were spies went in and brought out Rahab and her father and her mother and her brothers and all she had; they also brought out all her relatives and placed them outside the camp of Israel."

10. Joshua 6:25 "Rahab the prostitute lived in the midst of Israel to this very day." Matthew 1:5, 6 "Salmon was the father of Boaz by Rahab,

Boaz was the father of Obed by Ruth, and Obed was the father of Jesse. Jesse was the father of David the king."

11. Revelation 11:1–14 "And I will grant authority to my two witnesses. When they have finished their testimony, the beast will make war with them and kill them. After three and a half days, the breath of life from God came into them and they stood on their feet; and great fear fell upon those who were watching them. Then they went up to heaven in the cloud. In that hour there was a great earthquake, and a tenth of the city fell, seven thousand people were killed and the rest were terrified and gave glory to the God of heaven."

12. Revelation 19:14 "And the armies which are in heaven, clothed in fine linen, white and clean, were following him on white horses."

13. Revelation 19:15 "From his mouth comes a sharp sword, so that with it he may strike down the nations, and he will rule them with a rod of iron; and he treads the wine press of the fierce wrath of God, the Almighty."

14. Matthew 24: 36 "But of that day and hour no one knows, not even the angels of heaven, nor the Son, but the Father alone."

15. 1 Thessalonians 5:2–3 "For you yourselves know full well that the day of the LORD will come just like a thief in the night. While they are saying, 'Peace and safety!' then destruction will come upon them suddenly."

PSALM 22, 23, 24:

The Savior Shepherd King

I pulled the lamp closer to the edge of the scroll. The shadow of night had set upon me many hours ago, but I had found sleep to be a fleeting thing. I sat staring at the scroll before me trying hard to think of the words to write. My heart had been stirred deeply this night. The source of the stirring had seemed to reach more deeply than my heart. Certainly it was my soul that was touched. I had felt it before. This was not the first time I had been roused from my bed to put pen to paper. Even before I was king I had been touched more deeply than words can convey. It happened first when Samuel had anointed me as the next king. Even as the oil poured over my head and ran down my youthful chin I could feel the presence of the living God. I had felt my soul touched when as a shepherd

I had slain the bear or the lion that sought to bereave me of my sheep. I had experienced the very touch of God when in that valley I stood before the giant and called upon the Savior of Israel. I slew that giant with little more than a stone and I knew the hand of God was upon me (1).

Still this night was different. The room seemed cooler than normal so I took a tool and stirred the coals in the hearth. Bright orange sparks popped to life and with the breath of oxygen gave birth to fresh flame. It wasn't long after this that I went back to my chair and sat there quietly reflecting on how far the LORD had brought me and how favorably his hand had been toward me. I reached over and took hold of my harp. I thought that perhaps a strum or two would bring my scattered thoughts to focus. My calloused fingers plucked and played a most wonderful melody I had learned in my youth. I used to play it for Saul when he had been king. It always seemed to soothe his headaches (2). Yet, even as I played I knew this wasn't the answer.

I lay myself down on the thick rug spread across my floor and began to call out to my LORD and my God. I'm not sure if hours or minutes had passed but there on my face, late in the night, the answer came.

"David." The voice almost whispered to me. But I knew who it was.

"Yes, LORD?"

"David, I need you to sing for me tonight. I need you to sing of the Anointed One." My eyes looked up from the blank scroll that I had stretched out before me on the ground.

"What shall I sing, my LORD?"

The answer came back and my bones shook within me, "Sing of his death."

The words poured forth now as though the river had been unleashed from its holding place. The song broke my heart and cracked my voice. I sang them even as I wrote them.

"My God, my God, why have you forsaken me? O my God, I cry by day, but you do not answer; and by night, but I have no rest. Yet you are holy. In you our fathers trusted; they trusted and you delivered them. But I am a worm and not a man, a reproach of men and despised by the people. All who see me sneer at me. They cry out 'Let the LORD rescue you, because he delights in you.' The people surround me. Strong ones have encircled me. I am poured out like water. My bones are all out of joint; my heart is like wax; it is melted within me. My strength is gone and my tongue sticks to my jaws. You have laid me in the dust of death. These evildoers have pierced my hands and feet. I can count all of my bones. They divide my garments among them, and for my clothing cast lots" (3).

Trembling seized my heart and I wrung my hands in anguish. Tears flooded my face and deep cries of pain escaped my lips.

"No, O LORD! No! Certainly this shall not be!" My mind reeled with the song that I had just put on paper. The ink had scarcely begun to dry before my heart had been rend to pieces. The words that had leapt from my mouth now hung heavy in the air. I could not comprehend how this could be. How could the Anointed

One, the Savior of men, be despised? How could he be killed at the hand of evildoers? I had not yet begun to regain my composure when the voice came again.

"David." I fought to wipe the stinging tears from my eyes.

"Yes, LORD?" My voice rattled and shook.

"David, I need you to sing for me tonight. I need you to sing of the Anointed One." My eyes looked up from the scroll that told the story of death. My lips quivered.

"What shall I sing, my LORD?"

The answer came quickly and with no regard for my current state, "Sing of how he shall shepherd his people."

I did not understand how I could be asked to sing such a thing. I had just written of his death and *now* I was to write a song of him as a shepherd to his people? I had already written the end of the story. How could I then sing of him as a shepherd?

"I don't know if I can do it." The words were meant for my head alone but had somehow found their way from my throat and now echoed in the stillness of the room.

"I will give you the words," came the gentle reply.

I did know of shepherding. I had been a shepherd in my childhood and had kept careful watch over my father's sheep. I took up the pen and put it into the ink with trembling hand wondering what horrors would be spilled upon this page.

I began this way:

"The LORD is my shepherd, I shall not want."

I took strength from this first sentence and felt

my hand go back for more ink. My heart was filled with courage as I sang the next lines that were given to me.

"He makes me lie down in green pastures and leads me beside the still and quiet stream. He restores me and guides me in paths of righteousness for his sake. Though I may walk in the valley of the shadow of death I fear no evil for he is with me. He comforts me with his rod and staff. He prepares a table before me in the presence of my enemies and anoints my head with oil. He even overflows my cup. I know that goodness and mercy will follow me all the days of my life, and I will dwell in his house forever" (4).

As I finished these words, my heart that had been torn to pieces only moments before felt the cool balm of hope applied to its wounds. I pondered this more recent of the two Psalms. I was baffled at how one who had died could then be a shepherd to his people. But just the expectation of this possibility was like cool water to a parched tongue. Slowly my broken heart came back to life as I thought of the Anointed One being a shepherd to his people. We, the sheep of his pasture, being led by him to still waters and through green pastures. What a tremendous comfort to have a shepherd keep watch over me with a rod and a staff. Truly I should fear nothing even if my journey should take me to the very shadow of death for my shepherd is with me. As my eyes ran over the last line again I found myself singing in hearty agreement and with a great shout: "I will dwell in the house of the LORD forever!"

The shout fell back into silence and I sat there by

the gentle glows of the burning coals not quite ready to rouse myself from my place on the floor when I heard it again:

"David."

This time I was more eager to hear the voice.

"Yes, LORD?"

"David, I need you to sing for me tonight. I need you to sing of the Anointed One." I was excited to see what he would have me pen next so I spoke hurriedly.

"What shall I sing, my LORD?"

The answer came gentle and soft, "Sing of those who will be his and of his return to reign as King."

My hand shook with delight this time as I put the pen to the ink and then to the scroll. The words came quite suddenly.

"Who may stand in the LORD's holy place? Those with clean hands and pure heart, he who has not lifted up his soul to what is false and has not sworn deceitfully. He will receive righteousness from the God of his salvation. This is the generation of those who seek him.

"Lift up your heads, O gates, and be lifted up, O ancient doors, that the King of glory may come in! Who is the King of glory? He is the LORD strong and mighty, the LORD mighty in battle. The LORD of hosts, he is the King of glory" (5).

"Give me clean hands and a pure heart O God." The words poured forth from my mouth in a hasty tune. "O God, don't allow me to lift my soul to those things that are false, and let not my mouth swear deceitfully. Raise up a generation of those who would seek you with their whole heart."

Again my eyes were drawn to the last few lines I had written. I was elated to know that the King of glory would come back and set up his kingdom! My heart yearned to see the day!

"Come, LORD, come!" I sang this final chorus several more times my heart dancing within me and my feet soon following in like manner.

I waited for more words to come. I waited for the voice to give further instructions. The silence hung over the room like a blanket. I knew that this would not be the last time that the Spirit of God would take me from my bed and lay me on my face to pen a song. I decided to read once more the things that had found their way to the pages of my scroll. I was saddened by the death of the Anointed One but was glad to know that he would not find his end in death but rather would set himself up as a shepherd of his people. But even more thrilling to my heart was that I could ascend his holy hill, stand in his holy place, and see him come into his holy city to reign as King! I wasn't sure that I understood it all yet, but I knew that I had written of the Savior of men, the shepherd of the sheep, and the King of the holy people! I sang the songs that had been birthed in my heart this quiet evening.

I went to the window of my room and looked over the sleeping city of Jerusalem. I wondered if they knew that the Anointed One would die before he became their shepherd? I wondered if they ever thought of the day that the Anointed One would come and set himself up as King over his holy city and his holy people?

†

Jesus stood on a hill and looked over the sleeping city of Jerusalem. He had come as the Anointed One and they did not know it. He was preparing to die for them, and they would not receive it. He would seek to shepherd them, and they would not have it. He broke the silence of the night as he spoke, "Jerusalem, Jerusalem, who kills the prophets and stones those who are sent to her! How often I wanted to gather your children together, the way a hen gathers her chicks under her wings, but you were unwilling. Behold, your house is being left to you desolate! For I say to you, from now on, you will not see me until you say, 'Blessed is he who comes in the name of the Lord!'" (6).

The next few days passed quickly, and Jesus knew the time of death was upon him. Everything was getting ready to happen just as it had been written by the prophets of old. On the fourteenth day of the first month he celebrated the Passover with his disciples, as was the custom. After the supper he retired to a garden with a few chosen ones and prayed earnestly on behalf of those who would come to believe in him (7). Jesus had just finished praying when a band of soldiers led by Judas, the betrayer, came. They arrested the Christ and put him through several secret midnight trials, but the end had already been determined. In the morning they would hand him over to the Romans to be crucified.

The night of trials came with many beatings and the mocking of Jesus. The early morning saw Jesus flogged violently and his back lay open through the blows of the whip. A crown of thorns had been thrust upon his brow, and he carried the cross to Golgotha, which means "Place of the Skull." There they laid him upon the cross and drove spikes through his hands and feet (8). When Jesus had been crucified they raised the cross up and let it fall into the hole prepared for it. When it hit the bottom Jesus bounced and his shoulders dislocated (9). Those who gathered around the foot of the cross hurled insults at him and mocked him saying, "He trusts in God, so let God rescue him" (10). Jesus cried out with a loud voice, "My God, my God, why have you forsaken me?" (11). The priests and the scribes who had gathered to witness the death of their opponent were quickly reminded of the Psalm that David had penned so many years ago: "Father, forgive them; for they do not know what they are doing" (12). The words fell from the lips of Jesus even as the soldiers divided up his clothing among themselves and cast lots for his tunic (13). As his body grew weary and the life slipped from him, Jesus became thirsty, and his tongue clung to his mouth. Knowing that all things in Scripture had been fulfilled said, "I am thirsty" (14).

The Christ hung there on the cross breathing his final breaths but knowing that he would shortly be restored to life and would with great authority and power shepherd his people. He knew that he was being a good shepherd by laying down his life for his sheep (15). As the pounding of his heart rang in his ears, Jesus looked over those who had gathered. There was his mother and his beloved disciple. He knew that laying down his life was for them and for all the sheep of the various folds that he would bring together (16). He would not let death hold him in the grave, but after laying down his own life, he would take it up again (17).

Jesus paused again to catch his breath. They wouldn't understand it now but one day he would return as their King. One day he would return with his army at his side and he would rule on the earth (18). It was just a matter of time.

A soldier nearby heard the dying Savior speak of thirst and put a sponge full of sour wine on a stick and raised it to his dry bloody lips. When Jesus the Christ had received the wine, he said, "It is finished!" With that the King bowed his head and gave up his spirit (19).

Those around the cross who had loved him found their hearts rend to pieces and wept bitterly. But even as their heads were adorned with ashes of mourning and even as their faces were stained with tears, hope was being birthed. A shepherd was preparing to be born from the grave and this shepherd would finish the gathering of his flock and then rule them as their King. Then the hearts that had once been heavy would be made light. The voices that had moaned with sorrow would be raised in exaltation. Certainly those who had loved him would "dwell in his house forever" and would see "the King of Glory come in"!

The first two of the Kingly Psalms have been fulfilled and we anxiously await the third.

Scripture Index for Chapter Twelve

1. 1 Samuel 16:13 "Then Samuel took the horn of oil and anointed him in the midst of his brothers; and the Spirit of the LORD came mightily upon David from that day forward." 1 Samuel 17:34–35, 50–51 "Your servant was tending his father's sheep. When a lion or a bear came and took a lamb from the flock, and when he rose up against me, I seized him by his beard and struck him and killed him. Thus David prevailed over the Philistine with a sling and a stone, and he struck the Philistine and killed him."

2. 1 Samuel 16:23 "It came about whenever the evil spirit from God came to Saul, David would take the harp and play it with his hand; and Saul would be refreshed and be well, and the evil spirit would depart from him."

3. Psalm 22

4. Psalm 23

5. Psalm 24

6. This is a direct quote from Matthew 23:37–39.

7. John 17:9, 20 "I ask on their behalf; I do not ask on behalf of the world, but of those whom you have given me; for they are yours. I do not ask on behalf of these alone, but for those also who will believe in me through their word."

8. Psalm 22:16 "For dogs have surrounded me; a

band of evildoers has encompassed me; they have pierced my hands and my feet."

9. Psalm 22:14 "I am poured out like water, all of my bones are out of joint; my heart is like wax; it is melted within me." John 19:34 "But one of the soldiers pierced his side with a spear, and immediately blood and water came out."

10. Psalm 22:7–8, 17 "All who see me sneer at me; they separate with the lip, they wag the head, saying, 'Commit yourself to the LORD; let him deliver him; let him rescue him, because he delights in him. They look, they stare at me." Matthew 27: 39–44 "Those passing by were hurling abuse at him saying, 'If you are the Son of God, come down from the cross.' In the same way the chief priests also, along with the scribes and elders, were mocking him and saying, 'He saved others; he cannot save himself. He is the King of Israel, let him now come down from the cross and we will believe in Him. He trusts in God; let God rescue him now, if he delights in him.' The robbers who had been crucified with him were also insulting him with the same words."

11. Psalm 22:1 "My God, my God, why have you forsaken me?" Matthew 27:46 "About the ninth hour Jesus cried out with a loud voice, saying, 'My God, my God, why have you forsaken me?'"

12. Luke 23:34 "Jesus was saying, 'Father, forgive them; for they do not know what they are doing.' And they cast lots, dividing up his garments among themselves."

13. Psalm 22:18 "They divide my garments among them, and for my clothing they cast lots." John 19:23–25 "Then the soldiers, when they had crucified Jesus, took his outer garments and made four parts, a part to every soldier and also the tunic; now the tunic was seamless, woven in one piece. So they said to one another, 'Let us not tear it, but cast lots for it, to decide whose it shall be'; this was to fulfill the Scripture; 'They divided my outer garments among them and for my clothing cast lots.'"

14. Psalm 22:15 "My strength is dried up like a potsherd, and my tongue cleaves to my jaws; and you lay me in the dust of death." John 19:28–29 "After this, Jesus, knowing that all things had already been accomplished, to fulfill the Scripture, said, 'I am thirsty.' A jar full of sour wine was standing there; so they put a sponge full of the sour wine upon a branch of hyssop and brought it up to his mouth."

15. John 10:11 "I am the good shepherd; the good shepherd lays down his life for the sheep."

16. John 10:16 "I have other sheep, which are not of this fold; I must bring them also, and they will hear my voice, and they will become one flock with one shepherd."

17. John 10:17–18 "For this reason the Father loves me, because I lay down my life so that I may take it up again. No one has taken it away from me, but I lay it down on my own initiative. I have authority to lay it down, and I have authority to take it up again. This commandment I have received from my Father."

18. Revelation 19:11–16 "I saw heaven opened, and behold, a white horse, and he who sat on it is called Faithful and True, and in righteousness he judges and wages war. On his head are many diadems. The armies in heaven were following him on white horses. He will rule the nations with a rod of iron. On his robe and on his thigh he has a name written, 'King of Kings, and LORD of LORDS.'"

19. John 19:30 "Therefore when Jesus had received the sour wine, he said, 'It is finished!' and he bowed his head and gave up his spirit."

EZEKIEL 47, REVELATION 22:

The River of Life

Had it been more than a dream or a vision, it would have hardly been noticed by the casual viewer, but Ezekiel had the advantage of an angel to show him what he may have overlooked otherwise. The angel, tall and stately, glowed like polished bronze and took the prophet to the eastern side of the temple of the Most High God.

"Look there." The angel's voice seemed to vibrate Ezekiel to his core. At first Ezekiel didn't notice what the angel was indicating by his extended statuesque hand. He looked harder and furrowed his brow as he searched. The prophet noticed along the eastern wall a small tuft of green grass, alive and vibrant. He put his hand to the ground and found it wet. Was he supposed to be impressed by this? He looked back at his bronze tutor, unsure of what he should say or ask, but the gaze of the giant was fixed on this wet spot of earth. Ezekiel turned to look again and then he caught sight of a trickle of water working its way from under the foundation of the temple. Could this be what he was supposed to find? He dug his fingernails into the soft dark earth and drew it back toward his lap. The trickle of water snaked itself from underneath the wall of this most holy temple and filled the crevice Ezekiel had made.

"Where is this water coming from?" Ezekiel asked.

"Look there," the angel spoke again. The old prophet turned to look back at the wall of the temple and his eyes were opened to see that which is usually hidden from men's eyes. The wall became transparent like glass before him, his gaze fell beyond the pillars of bronze, and the great sea where the priests would wash themselves to land on the altar of sacrifice. It was beautiful and horrific all at once. The blood of atonement that had been sprinkled there stained the sides. Ezekiel thought of the many lambs that had given their bodies and spilled their scarlet life to cleanse the people who had sinned against the LORD. But the thing that drew his eye the most was the trickle of water from the wall of the temple that crawled across the floor and poured forth from the altar! Here is where the trickle began. It poured out of the altar and made its way across the floor of gold to be delivered from the temple on the eastern side and wet the soil at the prophet's feet (1).

"Look there." The voice of the angel caused Ezekiel to look up from the thread of water. His breath was taken from him as he saw that this trickle at his feet had become a great and wide river. The angel smiled at the surprise on the prophet's face and beckoned him to follow. Ezekiel walked through the cold water of the river and followed the angel fifteen hundred feet out, and the water covered his feet and ankles.

The angel continued forward. Fifteen hundred feet later, the water was deeper and now reached the knees of the prophet.

Still the angel pressed on.

Another fifteen hundred feet and the water encircled the waist of the prophet. He began to wonder at this a bit. He could feel the water of the river pushing him gently onward. He could feel his feet struggling to stay on the bottom. His tunic and robe had swallowed up the cold water, and he gasped as the icy river reached his chest.

Still the angel moved deeper.

Finally, just over a mile into the river, the angel stopped and looked to Ezekiel. The water was so deep now that there was no more walking forward, from here he could only swim (2). The great river stretched out as far as he could see, and he laughed. He didn't mean for it to be out loud and was a bit embarrassed that it had been. He turned to the angel to see if his bronze companion had noticed it. Assured that he hadn't been offensive to his host, he went back to pondering the wonder of it all. How could such a great river start as such a small insignificant trickle? Why should it come from the altar? What could this mean that such a mighty flowing river should cover the countryside? It seemed too much for him to take in.

"Son of man, have you seen this?" The shining host asked, almost as an afterthought, and turned back to shore (3).

Had he seen it? What kind of question was that? Of course he had seen it! He was standing chest deep in it! How could this mighty statue of a man ask such a question? But maybe...maybe the question wasn't so simple. Perhaps the question wasn't so much about what Ezekiel's eyes had seen but rather about what his mind had understood. The question wasn't about his eyes drinking in this vast watery continent, but rather "Ezekiel, have you understood this?" Did he perceive it? Did he know what this meant and what its purpose was? Had he understood the depth of it all? After pondering the question a bit more he had to admit that he was still puzzled and violently curious as to the meaning of this afternoon's journey, so he quietly and solemnly made his way back to the shore where his teacher stood waiting.

Ezekiel gained the shore and stood still. Dripping and cold he turned back to the crystal river to once again gaze upon the diamond brightness of it all. The angel smiled a bit knowing the surprise that would soon overcome the prophet. A surprise it was indeed! A resplendent forest had grown up on either side of the river. Great and magnificent trees overcame the banks, their branches borne low by the fruit on them (4). The coolness of the shadow fell across the shore.

Ezekiel's eyes were dazzled and his spirit was overcome by joy and childlike delight. What could this mean? What was it all for? He turned to his host and had scarcely formed the word with his lips when the answer came.

"These waters will flow down to the sea and the waters of the sea that are now dead shall be healed and made fresh. It will come about that every living creature, which swims and swarms wherever the river shall go, will live. There will be many fish, for this river will heal many waters and it will happen that wherever the river goes everything will live. The swamps and marshes that do not come in contact with the river shall not be healed nor made fresh but shall be a place of salt and death. Every place that the river goes trees shall spring up on the bank, first one side then the other. They shall be good for food and their leaves will never whither and they shall bear fruit. Their fruit shall never fall to the ground and it shall be for food and the leaves of the trees shall be for healing" (5).

Ezekiel blinked long and slow surveying the land before him again. The river was gone! The forest had been moved and the landscape before him returned to that which he had seen just this morning. He turned to ask the bronze man what he should do with all of this but he was gone. Ezekiel sat down on the ground, enthralled by the events of the day. He took a scroll from his robe and grappled for his pen and ink. He didn't know everything that this meant yet, but he knew he must record it for the future generations. He was certain that he had seen something high and lofty and those who would come after him would glean even more from this afternoon than he had.

Decades passed, building themselves into centuries, and centuries fell into millennia and the world moved on. Many had forgotten the words of Ezekiel and the afternoon he spent discovering a great and wide river whose origins were at the altar of sacrifice. Most had never even heard of that day and knew nothing of a river that brings with it life and healing. But there was one small preacher. He wasn't famous. His name wasn't known to any but the small flock that he had played shepherd to for the last thirty-five years. He stood before his people faithfully teaching the word of God week after week. This particular Sunday he dressed himself in his blue suit and put on the tie his wife had given him the Christmas before she passed away. He fiddled with the knot for a few minutes, wishing she were still here to fix it for him. His withered hands grasped the Bible he had preached from since he had left seminary, and he gave himself a final once-over in the mirror and made his way out the door and across the street to the small church. The sun poked its way through the many clouds that hung overhead and the coolness of fall filled his lungs. What a joy to know and serve the LORD! He made his way past the church sign that had today's sermon spelled out: "Ezekiel 47 and the River of Life." His deacon was just unlocking the front door as he walked up the ramp. It was easier for him than using the stairs these days.

Then the trumpeting of many great horns pierced

the air (6)! The old pastor looked skyward! His eyes blurred with tears of joy streaming down his face. His old, wrinkled face broke into a large, toothy smile. He held his hands high and jumped about.

"Hallelujah! Hallelujah!" he shouted. "The coming of the LORD is at hand! Hallelujah!"

So it was! Jesus had come on the clouds with glory, just as he said he would (7). He had come to take home all those who were his. It was time for the age of heaven!

The next step the pastor took was with renewed strength. He had been changed in a moment, in the twinkling of an eye. His old body had been exchanged for a new one. His feet danced upon the streets of gold. Instinctively he made his way to the throne of the Lamb of God, the one who had died for his sins. This was the one who had loved him so deeply. This was his Savior and his LORD. The renewed pastor followed the many into the great hall and beheld the throne of God and upon it sat the Ancient of Days, splendid with glory; his light illuminating the whole of this great and holy city (8). Next to that throne sat the throne of the Lamb, and Jesus seated on it. The preacher approached boldly to talk of things concerning this great and awesome salvation but as he did his eye was caught by a flood of water pouring out from underneath the throne of the Lamb of God. The great flood poured forth and wound its way across the expanse of heaven a great river, shining in a crystalline way. The river poured right down the middle of the street and on either side of this great river sprung up trees of every kind yielding fruit for food.

The leaves of the trees were given for the healing of the nations, and through this great river and the life that it brought the curse of sin had been removed (9)!

The preacher couldn't help but think of the sermon he had planned on preaching that very morning and stood amazed that he had not noticed before the great parallels between Ezekiel's river and this one that was here in heaven. Jesus noticed the long stares of this faithful man and pulled him near.

"Would you like to walk with me?" The Savior posed the question in the most compassionate way. The man nodded his approval, drinking in the very fragrance of heaven. The two walked along the river and through the fruit-heavy trees that engulfed its bank.

"What is it you want to ask?" the King and Savior asked.

The pastor thought for a moment then in a faint whisper, "I don't understand Ezekiel's river and how it relates to this great river here. I know that I should, but I suppose I've missed it over the years. Can you—would you teach me?"

Jesus smiled and looked over the river and began this way: "The river has always symbolized me. It symbolizes the life that I bring and healing from sin. Do you remember from where the river originated when Ezekiel saw it?"

"From the altar," the pastor spoke confidently.

"From the altar," Jesus repeated. "Don't you know that there can be no life, no forgiveness of sin, no healing without sacrifice (10)? Unless there had been an altar all mankind would have been destined for destruction. Every lamb laid on the altar, every drop of blood poured out was a symbol of the death I would die on the cross and of the blood that I would pour out for forgiveness of sins. Remember that I am the Lamb of God that takes away the sin of the world, so of course the river of life flows from the altar. It had to be this way. It was the only way it could be." Jesus paused a moment to see if the pastor was understanding and then continued, "And from where does the river flow here in heaven?"

"From your throne. The throne of the Lamb of God."

"From my throne. That's right. You see it's not enough that I died. Unless I am King, unless I conquer death to sit on the throne, there can be no life. The river of life flows from the altar because I am the sacrifice and from the throne because I am King. Unless I am your sacrifice and your King there can be no life, no healing, no removal of the curse of sin and death. Do not forget those swamps and marshes that Ezekiel wrote about. Those are the ones who remain separated from me, and for them there can be no life."

The pastor drank in deeply the things he was hearing and Jesus continued, "Do you remember the story of the exodus when the people were thirsty and Moses broke the rock and water poured out to give them life?" The preacher nodded. "Well I am the rock, which gives the water of life. Didn't Paul record 'All drank the same spiritual drink, for they were drinking from a spiritual rock and the rock was Christ' (11)? So you see then that I have always been the source of the river of life. Don't forget the Samaritan woman that I spoke with at the well. I told her that if she would ask me I would give her living water such that she would never thirst again. Furthermore, that if she drank of the water of life she would find that a well of water would spring up in her heart for eternal life (12). Did I not speak to the multitudes and tell them that 'If anyone is thirsty he should come to me and drink, and he who believes in me from his innermost parts will flow rivers of living water' (13)?

"So you see that I have always been the source of the river of life. I am the 'stream whose rivers make glad the city of God.' (14). It is those who come to me that shall drink their fill of the abundance of my house, for I will give them drink of the river of my delight. The fountain of all life lies with me (15). Don't forget Naaman and how, being dipped in the river, he was healed of his disease (16). Never forget how my Father rebuked that wicked generation that had forsaken the fountain of living water to pursue other sources of life. Ultimately they all died (17). I am the source for the river of life. Apart from me there is no life. You must come to the altar and to the throne to find healing for your soul. You must plunge yourself beneath the flood to be made clean and to find your forgiveness. In the river of my delights, you shall find life. Now teach the people!"

The old pastor looked at the Lamb of God with confusion on his face. Jesus just smiled back at him. Heaven before him began to fade away and as he lifted up his face, he found himself on his knees in prayer in his small, one-bedroom home. The picture of his wife sat on the dresser. Was it a dream? A vision? His soul stirred within him. He stood up and grabbed the tie that his wife had given him the Christmas before she died. He wished she were here to fix it for him. She was so much better at the knots than he was. He crossed the street and saw the church sign with the sermon title: "Ezekiel 47 and the River of Life." Underneath it was his name, "Pastor Ezekiel Todd."

That morning he stood in the pulpit and proclaimed to the people the truth of Jesus and the river of life that pours out from him.

"His sacrifice and his Kingdom are the source of all life!" He shouted in exaltation as he excitedly slapped the pulpit.

"Oh, sinner, there is life in no one else (18). Are you thirsty? Is your soul ready for the healing waters of life? Are you ready to be free from your sin and the curse of death? Turn to the Lamb who saves us! Call on the King who can give you life! You do not need to be beautiful. You need not find a way on your own. The way has been made for you! If you are thirsty, if you are in need of forgiveness, if you are in need of healing, to you I say, 'Ho! Every one who thirsts, come to the waters, and you who have no money come, buy and eat. Come buy wine and milk without money and without cost. Why do you continue to spend money for what is not bread and your wages for what does not satisfy? Listen carefully to me, and eat what is good, and delight yourself in abundance.' (19) Come to Jesus, the Lamb and the King, and find life for your soul."

The old preacher wept with these last words, pleading with his audience, and with tears and much joy, the pews were emptied and the whole of the congregation came to partake of the river of life.

Scripture Index for Chapter Thirteen

1. Ezekiel 47:1 "He brought me back to the door of the house; and behold, water was flowing from under the threshold of the house toward the east, for the house faced east. And the water was flowing down from under, from the right side of the house, from south of the altar."

2. Ezekiel 47:3–5 "He led me through water, water reaching the ankles. Again he measured a thousand cubits and led me through water reaching the knees. Again he measured a thousand and led me through water reaching the loins. Again he measured a thousand; and it was a river that I could not ford, for the water had risen, enough water to swim in, a river that could not be forded."

3. Ezekiel 47: 6 "He said to me, 'Son of man, have you seen this?' Then he brought me back to the bank of the river."

4. Ezekiel 47:7 "Now when I had returned, behold, on the bank of the river there were very many trees on the one side and on the other."

5. Ezekiel 47: 8–12 "These waters go out and flow into the sea, and the waters of the sea become fresh. It will come about that every living creature, which swarms in every place where the river goes, will live. And there will

be very many fish, for these waters go there and the others become fresh; so everything will live where the river goes. But its swamps and marshes will not become fresh; they will be left for salt. By the river on its bank, on one side and on the other, will grow all kinds of trees for food. Their leaves will not wither and their fruit will not fail. They will bear every month because their water flows from the sanctuary, and their fruit will be for food and their leaves for healing."

6. Matthew 24:31 "And he will send forth his angels with a great trumpet and they will gather together his elect from the four winds, from one end of the sky to the other." 1 Corinthians 15:52 "In a moment, in the twinkling of an eye, at the last trumpet; for the trumpet will sound, and the dead will be raised imperishable, and we will be changed."

7. Matthew 24:30 "And then the sign of the Son of Man will appear in the sky, and then all the tribes of the earth will mourn, and they will see the Son of Man coming on the clouds of the sky with power and great glory."

8. Revelation 21:23 "And the city has no need of the sun or of the moon to shine on it, for the glory of God has illumined it, and its lamp is the Lamb." Hebrews 4:16 "Let us draw near with confidence to the throne of grace, so that we may receive mercy and find grace to help in time of need."

9. Revelation 22:1–3 "Then he showed me a river of the water of life, clear as crystal, coming from the throne of God and of the Lamb, in the middle of its street. On either side of the river was the tree of life, bearing twelve kinds of fruit. The leaves of the tree were for the healing of the nations. There will no longer be any curse."

10. Hebrews 9:22 "Without the shedding of blood there is no forgiveness."

11. 1 Corinthians 10:4 "All drank from the same spiritual drink, for they were drinking from a spiritual rock which followed them; and the rock was Christ."

12. John 4:7–14 "If you knew the gift of God, and who it is who says to you, 'Give me a drink, ' you would have asked him, and he would have given you living water. Everyone who drinks of this water will thirst again; but whoever drinks of the water that I will give him shall never thirst; but the water I will give him will become in him a well of water springing up to eternal life."

13. John 7:37–39 "'If anyone is thirsty, let him come to me and drink. He who believes in me, as the Scripture said, "From his innermost being will flow rivers of living water."' But this he spoke of the Spirit, whom those who believed in him were to receive."

14. Psalm 46:4 "There is a river whose streams make glad the city of God, the holy dwelling places of the Most High."

15. Psalm 36: 8, 9 "They drink their fill of the abundance of your house, and you give them to drink of the river of your delights. For with you is the fountain of life and in your light we see light."

16. 2 Kings 5:14 "So Naaman went down and dipped himself seven times in the Jordan, according to the word of the man of God; and his flesh was restored like the flesh of a little child and he was clean."

17. Jeremiah 2:13 "For my people have committed two evils: they have forsaken me, the fountain of living waters, to hew for themselves cisterns, broken cisterns that can hold no water."

18. Acts 4:12 "There is salvation in no one else; for there is no other name under heaven that has been given among men by which we must be saved."

19. Direct quote of Isaiah 55:1–2

JONAH:

The One Appointed to Die That We Might Live

(With thanks to Colin Smith, Senior Pastor of The Orchard)

The pagan sailors trembled at the sight of the clouds on the horizon. They were all seasoned and had weathered many storms, but this one built so rapidly and seemed so ominous that every set of aged eyes was fixed on its coming. In a moment the violent breath of the gods was upon them, and they clambered to make fast the riggings and lower the sails. Their sturdy sea legs were overcome, and more than one man found himself thrown down hard upon the deck or slung headlong into the mast. There was no humor in it.

No one stopped to laugh at those who stumbled. Fear washed over each one and cold sweat soaked each brow. The waves grew to giant heights, and the ship seemed small by comparison. In a moment the tiny vessel would be at the crest of a mountainous wave, and in the following moment would be buried in a valley of water. The hammer of every wave and the violent burst of the wind seemed bent on sinking the ship and drowning each of the unfortunate sailors who had chosen to ride her.

When it was clear that the ship would be broken to pieces, the men began to fling their cargo overboard (1). All that would have been traded for money and all that would have made them rich men—or at least men of profit—had no value now. They could not buy their way out of this storm for they knew that this was more than a storm. This was the very judgment of God! When the last of the cargo had been sacrificed the men found their situation no better than when they had started. The light ship was tossed about as though the waves longed to play a catch with it.

Like the breaking of bones, the heavy planks of the ship began to pop and crack. The pagans knew that they were about to breathe their last. They each cried out to their own gods (2). They begged and pleaded for their lives. Some clung to the tiny statue they kept in their pocket. They kissed it, prayed to the small piece of stone, and implored it to save them. But it was silent as stones so often are. Others looked to the figurehead at the bow of the ship and with tears asked that they may be delivered, but the wooden figure simply stared vacantly forward. Every man was praying now to their god, but every man's god was nothing more than a piece of stone or a bit of wood. Every man's charm that he bore about his neck had failed.

They looked around and saw that one of their numbers was missing. The captain of the ship found the weary prophet below the deck, asleep on a pile of nets. The captain woke Jonah with a shake.

"Get up, man! How is it that you are sleeping at such a time as this? Call upon your god. Perhaps he will be concerned about us so that we will not die" (3). Jonah's sleep was cast from his eyes as the ship reeled again, and he found his stomach churning. The prophet did not have sea legs and clumsily climbed the stairs to the upper deck. The wind slapped him hard in the face, and the ocean spray stung his cheeks. The black clouds loomed like certain death all about them; and Jonah fell to his face, more from the storm and from weak legs than from humility.

The pagan sailors decided that they should cast the lot to determine who was to blame for this great calamity. One by one, the lot was cast until it landed at Jonah's feet. He was the guilty one!(4) The men looked to their guest. They didn't know much about him. He had joined them at their last port and had done so hastily.

"I serve the LORD God of heaven who made the sea and the dry land," Jonah shouted over the waves.

"What should we do with you that the seas may become calm for us?" the men asked resolutely for the sea was growing ever more tumultuous.

"Pick me up and cast me into the sea and then the sea shall become calm for you," came the reply

(5). The men looked at each other in disbelief and chose rather to put their backs to the oars. Each man took his place and rowed with all his might, straining hard with arms and shoulders and backs that were no match for the great storm (6). In protest the storm grew even heavier, and the once brave sailors came close to fainting. Finally when all they had done to save themselves had failed they cried out to the God of Jonah, "We earnestly pray, O Lord, do not let us perish on account of this man's life, and do not put innocent blood on us; for you, O Lord, have done as you pleased" (7).

With that, the men hastened to take hold of Jonah amid their cries of apology and cast him into the sea. Then the storm passed. The wind rushed off to some other place and the dark clouds parted and melted away. The waves settled to glass and the lion-like roaring of the tempest faded to quiet (8).

One man had been lost that many could be saved!

Jonah sunk beneath the waves like a stone. His robes made him heavy and he felt the pressure of the water wrap around him. The wrath and the fury of God were upon him and he was bearing the full weight of it. Far above him he could see the light of the sun playing upon the waves. At least the storm had broken. He was glad for that. Just as his lungs began to burn, just when the hand of death was upon him, a great fish swam past and took the prophet into his mouth. In a gulp, Jonah had gone from drowning to being at rest in the belly of a fish. This was his grave. This was his tomb. He would be buried here (9).

He did not yet know that he would be raised from the belly of this fish three days later to once again preach the coming of the Kingdom of God. To raise up a warning to the people that the wrath of God would be poured out on all who would not repent and turn to the LORD of salvation. (10)

Far above on the deck of the ship each man looked over the railing into the glassy water. They thought they had seen the prophet sink to the depths. They believed they had seen a great shadow pass in his direction, but now they were simply left staring at their own reflection on the surface. The small ripples the boat made in the now calm sea had broken the view of the deep. Silently the men turned to one another. Their gods of wood and stone dropped from their white fists and rattled around their feet. In a moment the men, in great fear, bowed themselves before the God of heaven and earth. They began in their rough way to offer the blood of sacrifice to the God who saves (11). Their lips that had moments before been filled with cries of fear were now overflowing with vows and praise to the God who would receive one man in their place. Their lives would be forever altered. One had gone down to the depths and had died in their place. One had borne the full measure of God's wrath that they might be saved from it. Now they knew life. Now they knew hope. This fearful afternoon had resulted in the saving of their souls.

†

Now here we are young sailors, on the ship that is our body. Or perhaps the salt of the sea has colored your hair white with time and the ship has grown heavy in the seas. Nonetheless the storm of the fury of God is building on the horizon. The tempest is making its way quickly to our vessel and we shall find that we don't have much time left in this world. Turn your back but a moment or let a blink linger on your eyes, and you will find that the Judgment is upon you. You have felt it already. Your legs quake beneath you and you find that all of your charms and all of your wealth cannot in this moment save your soul no matter how much confidence you place in them. Your stomach churns within you as you ponder the might of this magnificent God who will capsize your boat in a breath and cast you down to the depths. The wind and the rain leave stripes on your body like the whip as the sentence for your sins. Yet you know that is simply the prelude to the terrible weight of death you are about to face. The storm will splinter your tiny boat and the full measure of the sea of God's rage will be poured out on you. Imagine if you would that every drop of this great ocean would represent a single sin and that each of them together should drag you down and drown you and bury you and hide you in their infinite blackness.

Just then a solitary figure steps forward. He is not like you. He is not a sailor. He is the mouthpiece of the Living God.

"Cast me in and be saved," he says softly. You look at him in disbelief. Should he really die that you might live? Should he really bear the weight of your sin and your punishment that you might sail on? Initially you protest. You make further efforts to free yourself from the storm and its grip on you. You hasten to the oars thinking, *If I can just try harder certainly I can save myself.* God is offended by this thought and it causes his wrath to grow even more violent around you. You have already turned to all the other gods, those little bits of powerless stone and wood and found them to be silent and lacking in power. The man stands in your midst again.

"Cast me in and be saved."

Your mind wrestles with it. *How could that be fair? He is innocent. Wouldn't I be further guilty to have him die for me?* Still as the storm raged on it was clear that there was only one option. We find ourselves identified with those sailors of old, those pagan sinners who were on the verge of death. We have taken our hands and laid hold of the Savior of all men. His name is Jesus Christ. And so we might have life, we have cast him down to the depths by our own sins. He would stay there, buried, for three days. But in all power he would be raised back to life to proclaim the message of the living God (12).

Do not miss this. One has died in your place. By Jesus' death you have found life. We must be careful that we don't follow every example to its logical conclusion. We know that Jonah was guilty while Jesus was not. We know that Jonah was the cause of

God's judgment while it is our sin that has stirred up the wrath of God. We know that the men pleaded that they would not be guilty of the blood of Jonah as they slew him, while the voices of those who crucified Christ shouted, "His blood be on us and our children"(13).

Yet, Jonah did die that others might be saved from God's wrath, and so it is with Christ. Jonah did spend three days and three nights in the depth of the grave, as did Christ. Jonah was raised to preach the Kingdom of God and saw many souls saved, just as Jesus was raised to testify to the Kingdom of heaven that you and I might be saved.

Don't miss it.

Do you see the clouds building? "It is appointed for men to die once and after this comes judgment" (14).

Will you face the fury of God's wrath yourself? Will you find your charms and your gods too weak to save you in your time of need? Will you find all of your cargo and riches could not buy your freedom? Or will you rely on him who saved you from the coming wrath; the one appointed to die that we might live (15)?

Scripture Index for Chapter Fourteen

1. Jonah 1:5 "The sailors threw the cargo which was in the ship into the sea to lighten it for them."

2. Jonah 1:5 "The sailors became afraid and every man cried to his god."

3. Jonah 1:5–6 "But Jonah had gone below into the hold of the ship, lain down and fallen sound asleep. So the captain approached him and said, 'How is it that you are sleeping? Get up, call on your god. Perhaps your god will be concerned about us so that we will not perish.'"

4. Jonah 1:7 "Each man said to his mate, 'Come let us cast lots so we can learn on whose account this calamity has struck us.' So they cast lots and the lot fell on Jonah."

5. Jonah 1:9, 12 "He said to them, 'I am a Hebrew, and I fear the LORD God of heaven who made the sea and the dry land. Pick me up and throw me into the sea. Then the sea will become calm for you, for I know that on account of me this great storm has come upon you.'"

6. Jonah 1:13 "However, the men rowed desperately to return to land but they could not, for the sea was becoming even stormier against them."

7. Jonah 1:14 "Then they called on the LORD and said, 'We earnestly pray, O LORD, do not let us perish on account of this man's life and do not put innocent blood on us; for you, O LORD, have done as you have pleased.'"

8. Jonah 1:15 "So they picked up Jonah, threw him into the sea, and the sea stopped its raging."

9. Jonah 1:17 "And the LORD appointed a great fish to swallow Jonah, and Jonah was in the stomach of the fish three days and three nights."

10. Jonah 2:10, 3:1–3 "Then the LORD commanded the fish, and it vomited Jonah up onto the dry land. Now the word of the LORD came to Jonah the second time, saying, 'Arise, go to Nineveh the great city and proclaim to it the proclamation which I am going to tell you.' So Jonah arose and went to Nineveh according to the word of the LORD."

11. Jonah 1:16 "The men feared the LORD greatly, and they offered a sacrifice to the LORD and made vows."

12. Matthew 12: 40 "Just as Jonah was three days and three nights in the belly of the sea monster, so will the Son of Man be three days and three nights in the heart of the earth." 1 Corinthians 15:3–6 "Christ died for our sins according to the Scriptures, and he was buried, and he was raised on the third day according to the Scriptures, he appeared to Cephas, then to the

twelve. After that he appeared to more than five hundred brethren at one time."

13. Matthew 27:25 "And all the people said, 'His blood shall be on us and on our children!'"

14. Hebrews 9:27 "It is appointed for men to die once and after this comes judgment."

15. Romans 5:9 "Having now been justified by [Christ's] blood, we shall be saved from the wrath of God through him."

GENESIS 14, REVELATION 5:

*The King of Salem and the
Lion and the Lamb*

Abram returned from battle weary and worn. He had rescued his nephew Lot from those who had taken him as a slave. Not only that, but he had rescued all the people of the region who had been taken into captivity. He wasn't looking for honor or fame. As he returned with all the people and possessions the king of Salem came out to meet with him. This king was named Melchizedek and he was the first priest of the Most High God. He blessed Abram thus proving that he was greater than mighty Abram for the lesser is always blessed by the greater (1).

Melchizedek, his name means "king of righteous-ness" and he was king of Salem. Salem means "peace." (2) Salem would also eventually become the city called Jerusalem. This Melchizedek was by his very nature "king of righteousness" but he became "king of peace." This priest of the Most High God, this king is a pic-ture of Jesus as the author of Hebrews points out to us several times (4). For truly Jesus is our Priest and our King. Jesus is by his nature "king of righteous-ness." That is to say that Jesus is by nature lion. But Jesus became "king of peace" for us. That is to say that Jesus became lamb. You cannot divorce the lion from the lamb. If you do not fall under the blood of the lamb you will fall before the tooth and claw of the lion. Though Jesus came to the earth at first as a lamb, gentle and in a manger, the servant of men, when he returns he does so as a King. Heaven will open up and Jesus will come forth riding a white horse. They shall call Jesus "Faithful and True" and he will judge and make war righteously. His eyes will gleam like torches of fire, and on his head will be the crowns of all the kingdoms of the earth. His robe will be dipped in blood and they will call him "The Word of God." All the armies in heaven will follow at his heels while out of his mouth will come a sharp sword. With it he will strike down the nations. He will rule them with a rod of iron and tread the winepress of the fierceness and wrath of God Almighty. Written on his thigh will be the name "King of Kings, and LORD of LORDS" (3).

✝

In another place and many years later, there was a lion laying lazily in the shade of a desert tree. He was a faithful creature of God. The word of the LORD came to that lion in the late afternoon.

"Lion, a prophet of mine has disobeyed me. I have warned him to be obedient. I require righteousness from those who would endeavor to serve me. He will be passing by on the road that leads down from Bethel to Judah. When he comes by on his donkey, I want you to strike him down for his sin."

The lion twitched and flopped his tail around in the dust and, with a yawn and a stretch, rose up from the ground. The quiet pads of his feet tread the desert grass gently down. He moved silent like the wind over the hills and sand. The eyes of the great and fearsome beast glistened in the light as they searched the road, waiting for the one he should pour out God's fury on.

An hour passed and the sun sank a little lower in the sky, but eventually came a lone man around the bend on a donkey.

"This is the one," the LORD whispered into the ear of the lion.

Like a tightly wound spring set loose the lion sprung up from the dirt and dust forcing a cloud of debris into the air. His clawed feet pounded the ground effortlessly as he closed the gap between himself and the one who had sinned against the righteous God.

The prophet didn't turn from his course.

With muscled form bending and twisting and

flashing gold in the sun, the lion let out a roar that was far from weak. It rang so violently through the air that it charged upon the ears of the prophet and touched his blood with an icy hand.

There was a blur of yellow, a scream cut short, and a flash of red. The brutality of it was painted across the ground. But the lion had not been sent here to devour. He had been brought here simply to destroy. Having upheld the righteous will of God, he stood placidly next to the body. The donkey was frozen in fear, standing on the other side of the prophet's corpse. His eyes were wide and his nostrils flared with panic. He nervously pranced on the ground, but the lion was not there for his appetite. The Lord who had called him would later provide his food. So he left the donkey and the corpse alone.

The righteousness of God was satisfied (5).

†

Many years passed. Kings came and went, but Israel refused to follow the will of the living God. Once during a great battle, there was a lion resting in her cave. The day was hot and the coolness of this sanctuary brought refreshment. On this day God called to this lion.

"Lion, a prophet of mine has disobeyed my command. My righteousness demands righteousness. I need you to destroy this wicked one."

The head rose up from the stony floor and the heavy tongue licked at the spear-like teeth. Emerging from the darkness and into the sun, the lion moved from rock to rock and into the battle. Bodies were scattered everywhere. Those who were living were busy looting the dead. A few vultures hopped in an uneasy manner away from the corpse they were robbing. They were bowing to the greater predator, but this lion had no desire to devour these fallen ones. Once she had passed by, the vultures called to each other and fell upon their buffet again like a shadow.

"Lion," the LORD spoke again, "the wicked prophet is speaking to a righteous prophet. The moment the wicked one departs from the righteous one, I want you to strike him down. Do not touch the righteous prophet, for certainly I treat the righteous and the wicked differently."

As the lion walked among the men she became increasingly agitated. But in time she came upon two men speaking in rapid tones. These were the two she had been told about.

One of the men spoke to the other, "Because you have not listened to the voice of the LORD, as soon as you leave me, a lion will kill you." The lioness crouched low to the ground and drug herself forward in the warm sand, her black claws shining like flint stones. When the wicked man departed the company of the righteous, she flung herself forward. There was no warning. No roar. Muscles, sinews, teeth, and claws worked in a bloody orchestra and struck down the one who had disobeyed the righteous King.

Some had stopped and stared, but a moment later she was gone.

The righteousness of God was satisfied (6).

†

Years of rebellion plagued the nation of Israel. They had so hardened their hearts that the LORD had sent them into captivity. Those who refused to bow to God and traded the Savior for idols made by hands were now in a war-torn land. Other nations had come and had removed them from their homes and cities and led them away in chains to be slaves. Those who had fallen upon the Israelites now possessed their cities. The Assyrians brought people from all over the world to dwell in the homes of those who had been called by the name of God. However, at the beginning of their living there, they did not fear the LORD.

A pride of lions was residing along the cool banks of the Jordan River. It had been a day of lapping up the cold waters and keeping the flies at bay, but now the LORD was speaking to them.

"Lions, wicked people have moved into Israel that do not know me nor do they serve me. They bow down to idols of wood and stone. They have transgressed my righteousness. Go and kill some of them so that they might know that God is still in Israel."

The king of the pride, with a roar, brought the lions to their feet. The group started off into the setting sun to bring God's judgment upon the wicked strangers settling in Samaria. A ghostly, silent group of death-bringers moved across the ground with a taste for blood on their tongues. The sun surrendered and fell to the ground, and darkness pulled his robe over the earth. The stars and moon shone brilliantly upon these determined soldiers. Wild sheep and goats bleated in fear as the pack numbering greater than twenty made their way through the folds.

Early in the morning when the dew had freshly fallen upon the grass, the tireless assassins crested a hill and looked over a sleepy city below.

Here a lion slipped into a house through the open window.

There, a lion crept upon the soldier walking the street.

Just beyond the gates a lonely walker carrying a pot for water was being stalked.

Then the wrath of God fell.

In a darkened bedroom, the lion with great fury and flashing fang crushed the skull of the sleeper. Piercing screams shook the stillness of daybreak and the soldier turned in time to see a heavy beast suspended in mid-leap with razor talons extended and glistening teeth bared. The weight was so heavy upon his chest, the blow so forceful, that before he had hit the ground he was unconscious. It would prove to be a blessing as the lion flayed him for his wickedness. Outside the city a water pot broke to pieces and dust is drowned. A quick eye sees the mighty harbinger of death dragging a lifeless body through the grass. A sandal sprinkled red and lying at the side of the road tells a story too horrific for children. Another father left without a daughter, another orphan created in a moment.

And so it was all over Samaria. It wasn't just one pride, not just one city. All over the wicked country souls were being slain for the lack of knowing the Lord, for the lack of serving him.

The righteousness of God was satisfied (7).

†

A few years later, a righteous man named Daniel was falsely accused of wrongdoing. The law was clear. He must be thrown to the lions. The king fought hard to save him, but not even he was above the law. The stone was removed from the mouth of the den and a shaft of light fell heavily into the pit. Daniel was cast down and tumbling landed hard on the stony ground. Above him the circle of daylight was eclipsed as the scraping stone was pushed back into place. His nostrils were offended by the stench of manure, foul beasts, and death. He sat up and blinked at the inky darkness. A crack of light fell upon the floor, a mere sliver of hope. Daniel heard the shuffle of a heavy body to his left. On his right he could distinguish at least two other lions shuffling in the black. The hair rose sharply on his neck as he felt the warm wet breath fall on his face. He blinked harder hoping to perceive this stranger. The stink of decay bathed him, but there was no claw, not a single tooth buried itself in his soft skin. A roar vibrated off of his chest and his heart seemed to thunder. It had just been seconds but had seemed much longer.

Irradiant light filled the small tomb. Daniel's eyes shut instinctively, finding the glow too powerful for eyes just adjusted to the dark. An angel stood in the room. He was tall and strong. A sword was in his hand gleaming brightly. With this sudden intrusion, the lions retreated like scared kittens pushing themselves against the rocks trying to find a shadow that could conceal them. Daniel looked about and saw that there were far more than he had expected and moved slowly toward the angel of God.

"Daniel, you have been found innocent before God and have done no wrong to the king, so I have come to shut the lion's mouths," the angel's voice trumpeted and then he was gone.

Daniel was again thrust into blindness for the darkness that rushed upon him. He heard the lions stir again. He could feel them brushing past him, even a gentle bump pushed him sideways. A warm body pressed into him, and a heavy head buried in his chest. The coarse hair scratched his face, but Daniel was at peace. He was righteous before the LORD, so the lions could not touch him. They would not. They were God's lions and would not strike down a holy one.

The morning found Daniel at rest, and the stone was pushed away, flooding the den with fresh morning air and powerful light. The king rescued Daniel, lifting him from the pit of lions.

There were three wicked men who had been the ones to falsely accuse Daniel. The king's fury burned hot against them. He had the men, their wives, and their children brought and cast into the lion's lair, but the lions would not be so accommodating this time around. God had spoken to them and had roused them from their slumber and loosed their jaws. The three men and their families tumbled over each other into the open mouth of God's judgment. Before their bodies could reach the floor, the lions had overpowered them and crushed every bone in their bodies. The sound was a stomach-turning blend of screams, roars, and breaking bones.

God had once again made a distinction between the righteous and the wicked. He had once again withheld judgment and wrath from the innocent and had with great rage poured them out on those who were found to be in sin.

The righteousness of God was satisfied (8).

†

God isn't only wrath. To be sure, he will pour out his wrath on all who are far from him, on all who are wicked. But there is hope and mercy and grace. Our sins can be removed from us. The disease of sin can be ripped from our deceitful heart and we can be made clean. Our filthy garments of sin can be traded for beautiful garments, pure and white, made clean by the blood of the Lamb (9).

The animal had lived in the Garden of Eden full of joy and delight. God walked in the garden in the cool of the evening and would talk with the man and woman he had made and placed there.

One day a shadow fell across the bliss of this paradise. The man and woman had sinned against God and broken his command. He had promised death! The animal was nearby grazing when the LORD appeared again radiant in glory and beautiful in splendor like polished bronze or glowing metal.

God spoke to the sinners. His wrath was certainly going to be poured out. His fury would only be satiated by blood, but God did not strike down the two in the garden. Instead he made his way to the grazing animal.

With one swift blow the sacrifice fell dead under the mighty hand of God, his blood soaking the soil. God had determined to save his creation by killing one in their place (10).

✝

Abraham was a righteous man who was submitting himself to the LORD. The LORD had spoken to him, "Abraham, take your only son to a place I will show you, and kill him there for me."

Abraham obeyed.

He had brought his son, Isaac, to a mountain in the region of Moriah and had built an altar. He had bound his son with chords and had laid him on the altar. He had raised the knife up in the air, preparing to spill the blood of his child.

But the LORD spoke, "Abraham, Abraham! Do not lay a hand on the boy. Look there in the bushes."

Abraham lifted his eyes and saw a ram caught in the thicket by his horns. The ram must have thought it a peculiar sight. To see a man and a boy come up to the top of the mountain with beads of sweat pouring down their faces. The older one began to accumulate stones and stack them into a heap. The younger one was stacking the wood on the stones. The ram saw the older one speak to the younger one and the color drained from each face as terror flooded the eyes of the child. There was a long embrace as the two wept. The father tied the boy securely and took him up in his arms holding him firmly to his chest just before he laid his son on the wood. The father was just about to slay his son when a voice called out to him from heaven. The father stopped! A moment later the father turned and looked at the thicket. The ram had been seen!

"I'm here. Please let me loose," the ram bleated in a language unknown to men. Abraham came and gently turned the head of the ram and untangled him from the brambles. The ram was so tired that he bleated again in excitement when the father picked him up and carried him back to where the boy was laying. Abraham took the lad from the altar and cut the bindings loose. Isaac knelt and hugged the neck of the ram. The ram loved it and gave the child a lick or two.

Abraham then took the ram and binding his feet laid him on the altar. With a bleat of fear, a flash of steel, and a spray of blood all was silent. The ram had been provided so that the child could be spared. God had provided a sacrifice in place of the boy. And so it is that we who believe are called children of God and, instead of slaying us, our Father God has provided a sacrifice on our behalf (11).

†

Moses had given the instructions for the Passover. In obedience and for fear of death, people went to their flocks on the tenth day of the first month and took a young lamb without blemish. The lamb was taken into the house and cared for. He was loved and fed. He was cherished, but he was cherished because it was he who would be slain in place of those who dwelt in the house. Each person in the home looked upon the lamb praying that his blood would be sufficient to save. After a time of living among the people the lamb was brought to a place outside of the house. The father took the lamb with a firm grip and forced the head over a bowl. With a swift stroke the blood was spilled and collected. The father was pleased to do this for only being covered by the blood of this lamb could salvation be given. All across the slave city in Egypt lambs were killed so that others may live. So it was that Jesus lived among man, but eventually he was led outside the city and was crushed on our behalf. Furthermore, the Father God was pleased to do it, for it meant salvation for many people (12).

Every morning and every evening the High Priest would take a lamb and bring it before the altar of the LORD. With great precision the priest would slay the lamb and pour the blood out by the altar on the north side. The priest would then take some of the blood and sprinkle it on all sides of the altar. The lamb would then be cut and arranged on the altar and burned there as a pleasing aroma to the LORD, and the sins of the people would be atoned for (13).

And a lamb was slain to consecrate the priests so that they could come in and out and minister before the LORD. Its blood was placed on the right ear, right thumb, and right big toe of those to be set apart as holy. The blood made them holy (14).

†

A lamb was slain for the leper when he was being made clean. The blood of this sacrifice was placed on the right ear, right thumb, and right big toe of those who were to be cleansed. The blood made them clean (15).

When Jesus came walking on the earth and was passing by it was with great wisdom that John the Baptist said, "Behold the Lamb of God that takes away the sin of the world" (16). For certainly we are all filthy lepers only made clean by the blood of Jesus. We are all priests of God set apart as holy by the blood of Jesus (17). The blood has been sprinkled on us and taken away our sin. The blood of Jesus has been painted on the doors of our hearts, and we have been redeemed like the firstborn in Egypt. Jesus was the sacrifice in our place, for we are called the children of God. And Mount Moriah, where Abraham sacrificed that ram would be where the great temple of God should stand, and it would be the region where Christ was crucified on our behalf. It was his blood that spared us and made us children. When the creator should have put us to death he instead slew an innocent one so that we should be preserved.

Jesus' blood in place of mine.

Jesus' life for mine.

John the revelator was caught up in a vision of heaven. The splendor and beauty overcame him. Sorrow swept over him when no one was found worthy to open the scroll. An elder spoke to him in a thunderous voice, "Behold the lion of the tribe of Judah. He can open the scroll" (18).

John turned to look upon the lion and through tearful eyes beheld a lamb looking as though it had been slain. When the slaughtered (for that is what the word slain means) lamb took hold of the scroll all of heaven erupted into spontaneous worship. The entire number of all the saints fell down before him and cried out in such a loud voice that all of heaven shook, "Worthy is the Lamb that was slain to receive power and riches, wisdom, might, honor, glory, and blessing. To him who sits on the throne, and to the Lamb, be blessing, honor, glory, and dominion forever and ever" (19).

Make no mistake about it. Jesus has always been the lion of righteousness, but when he came to us at first, he came as the lamb of peace. When he comes again, it will be as both the lion and the lamb. His wrath and fury will be poured out on all who are not his, and his mercy and peace will be poured out on all who name the name of Jesus. The Lamb will return with the wrath of the Lion and the wicked will beg to be hidden from it (20). But those who have washed their robes in the blood of the Lamb will encircle his throne declaring in loud song, "Salvation belongs to the Lamb who sits upon the throne." The Lamb will forever be their shepherd and will guide them to living waters to drink (21).

The blood of the Lamb will finally overcome the great enemy: the devil, that foul serpent.

The wedding in heaven will be glorious as Jesus

the Lamb brings the redeemed, the saints, the church, the bride, the children, the firstborn, and the saved near to himself (22).

There will be no more temple, for Jesus the Lamb is the temple. There will be no more sun or moon or stars, for the glory of the Lamb will illuminate all of heaven (23).

Only those whose names have been found written in the Lamb's book of life, only those who have been saved by his blood, shall find themselves there (24). The river of life will flow from his throne and the curse will be lifted forever (25).

Jesus!

All of history would have you know him! He will be your destruction or he will be your salvation!

You will be saved by his blood or find your blood spilled by his sword.

There is yet time to know this Jesus. The blood of the Lamb can still save you. You need not fear the roar of the Lion. It is not the saved that the Lion is seeking, nor is it the righteous that he longs to crush. His tooth and claw have been reserved for the wicked.

Do you know this King of Righteousness?

Do you fear this Lion?

Do you know this King of Peace?

Do you love this Lamb?

Do you know this Creator?

Do you know this River of Life?

Do you know the Bread of Life?

Do you know the sweet tree or the stricken rock?

Do you know the scarlet cord?

Do you know the ladder to heaven?

Do you know this overlooked deliverer?

Do you know this Savior?

Do you know this Shepherd?

Do you know the Curse Bearer?

Do you know the One appointed to die in our place?

Do you know the One lifted up that we might live?

Do you know this ark of salvation?

His name is Jesus!

Scripture Index for Chapter Fifteen

1. Genesis 14:18 "And Melchizedek king of Salem brought out bread and wine; now he was a priest of God Most High. He blessed Abram."

2. Hebrews 6:19–7:17 "Jesus has entered as a fore-runner for us, having become a high priest forever according to the order of Melchizedek. For it is attested of [Christ], 'You are a priest forever according to the order of Melchizedek.'" *See specifically Hebrews 5:5–6, Hebrews 7:1–3, 11–17.*

3. Revelation 19:11–16 "I saw heaven opened, and behold, a white horse, and he who sat on it is called Faithful and True, and in righteousness he judges and wages war. His eyes are a flame of fire, and on his head are many diadems; and he is clothed with a robe dipped in blood, and his name is called the Word of God. The armies, which are in heaven, clothed in fine linen, white and clean, were following him on white horses. From his mouth comes a sharp sword, so that with it he may strike down the nations, and he will rule them with a rod of iron; and he treads the wine press of the fierce wrath of God the Almighty. And on his robe and on his thigh he has a name written, 'King of kings, and LORD of LORDS.'"

4. Hebrews 7:1–2 "For this Melchizedek, king of Salem, priest of the Most High God, was first of all, by the translation of his name, king of righteousness, and then also king of Salem, which is king of peace."

5. 1 Kings 13:1–33 "'Because you have disobeyed the command of the LORD your body shall not come to the grave of your fathers.' Now when the prophet had gone, a lion met him on the way and killed him, and his body was thrown on the road, with the donkey standing beside it; the lion was also standing beside the body. The lion had not eaten the body nor torn the donkey."

6. 1 Kings 20:26–36 "Now a certain man of the sons of the prophets said to another by the word of the LORD, 'Please strike me.' But the man refused to strike him. Then he said, 'Because you have not listened to the voice of the LORD, behold, as soon as you have departed form me, a lion will kill you.' And as soon as he had departed form him a lion found him and killed him."

7. 2 Kings 17:7–41 "The king of Assyria brought men from Babylon and from Cuthah and from Avva… and settled them in the cities of Samaria in place of the sons of Israel. At the beginning of their living there, they did not fear the LORD; therefore the LORD sent lions among them which killed some of them."

8. Daniel 6:16–28 "Daniel was brought and cast into the lions' den. A stone was brought and laid over the mouth of the den. In the morning the king spoke to Daniel, 'Has your God, whom you constantly serve, been able to deliver you from the lions?' Then Daniel spoke to the king, 'O king, live forever! My God sent his angel to shut the lions' mouths and they have not harmed me, inasmuch as I was found innocent before him; and also toward you, O king, I have done no wrong.' So Daniel was taken up out of the den and no injury whatever was found on him, because he had trusted in his God. Then the king gave orders, and they brought those men who had maliciously accused Daniel, and they cast them, their children and their wives into the lions' den; and they had not even reached the bottom of the den before the lions overpowered them and crushed all of their bones."

9. Zechariah 3:1–5 "God spoke and said to those who were standing before him, 'Remove the filthy garments from him.' Again he said to him, 'See, I have taken your iniquity away from you and will clothe you with festal robes.'"

10. Genesis 3:21 "The LORD God made garments of skin for Adam and his wife, and clothed them." *Remember the chapter on Genesis 3.*

11. Genesis 22:1–19 "Abraham built the altar there and arranged the wood, and bound his son Isaac and laid him on the altar, on top of the

wood. Abraham stretched out his hand and took the knife to slay his son. But the angel of the LORD called to him from heaven and said, 'Abraham, Abraham! Do not stretch out your hand against the lad, and do nothing to him.' Then Abraham lifted his eyes and looked, and behold, behind him a ram caught in the thicket by his horns; and Abraham went and took the ram and offered him up for a burnt offering in the place of his son. Abraham called the name of that place The LORD Will Provide, as it is said to this day, 'In the mount of the LORD it will be provided.'" *Don't forget that this is the same mountain where the temple and crucifixion will take.*

12. Exodus chapters 11–12 cover the Passover. Remember the earlier chapter about the Passover.

13. Exodus 29:38–39 "Now this is what you shall offer on the altar: two one-year-old lambs each day, continuously. The one lamb you shall offer in the morning and the other lamb you shall offer at twilight."

14. Leviticus 8:2–24 "Moses took the second ram of ordination and slaughtered it and took some of its blood and put it on the lobe of Aaron's right ear, and on the thumb of his right hand and on the big toe of his right foot. He also had Aaron's sons came near and put the blood on them."

15. Leviticus 14:13–14 "Next [the priest] shall slaughter the male lamb in the place where they slaughter the sin offering and the burnt offering, at the place of the sanctuary—for the guilt offering. The priest shall then take some of the blood of the guilt offering, and the priest shall put it on the lobe of the right ear of the one to be cleansed [of leprosy], and on the thumb of his right hand and on the big toe of his right foot."

16. John 1:29 "The next day he saw Jesus coming to him and said, 'Behold, the Lamb of God who takes away the sin of the world!'"

17. 1 Peter 2:9 "But you are a chosen race, a royal priesthood, a holy nation, a people for God's own possession, so that you may proclaim the excellencies of him who has called you out of darkness to his marvelous light."

18. Revelation 5:4–6 "I was weeping greatly because no one was found worthy to open the book or to look into it; and one of the elders said to me, 'Stop weeping; behold, the Lion that is from the tribe of Judah, the Root of David, has overcome so as to open the book and its seven seals.' And I saw between the throne and the elders a Lamb standing, as if slain."

19. Revelation5: 7–14 "When he had taken the book the four living creatures and the twenty-four elders fell down before the Lamb. And

they sang a new song, saying, 'Worthy are you
to take the book and break its seals; for you
were slain, and purchased for God with your
blood men from every tribe and tongue and
people and nation. You have made them to be
a kingdom and priests to our God; and they
will reign upon the earth.' Then the voice of
many angels around the throne; myriads of
myriads, thousands of thousands, said with a
loud voice, 'Worthy is the Lamb that was slain
to receive power and riches and wisdom and
might and honor and glory and blessing. To
him who sits on the throne, and to the Lamb,
be blessing and honor and glory and dominion
forever and ever.'"

20. Revelation 6:16 "And they said to the mountains and the rocks, 'Fall on us and hide us
from the presence of him who sits on the
throne, and from the wrath of the Lamb.'"

21. Revelation 7:9–17 "After these things I looked,
and behold, a great multitude which no one
could count, from every nation and all tribes
and peoples and tongues, standing before the
throne and before the Lamb, and they cry out
with a loud voice, saying, 'Salvation to our
God who sits on the throne, and to the Lamb.'
And all the angels were standing around the
throne and around the elders and the four
living creatures; and they fell on their faces
before the throne and worshiped God, saying,
'Amen, blessing and glory and wisdom and

thanksgiving and honor and power and might, be to our God forever and ever. Amen.' One of the elders spoke to me and said, 'These are the ones who come out of the great tribulation, and they have washed their robes and made them white in the blood of the Lamb.'"

22. Revelation 19:7, 9 "'Let us rejoice and be glad and give the glory to him, for the marriage of the Lamb has come and His bride has made herself ready.' Then he said to me, 'Write, "Blessed are those who are invited to the marriage supper of the Lamb.""'" Revelation 21:9 "Then one of the seven angels spoke to me saying, 'Come here, I will show you the bride, the wife of the Lamb.'"

23. Revelation 21:22–23 "I saw no temple there, for the LORD God the Almighty and the Lamb are its temple. And the city has no need of the sun or of the moon to shine on it, for the glory of God has illumined it, and its lamp is the Lamb."

24. Revelation 21:27 "And nothing unclean, and no one who practices abomination and lying, shall ever come into it, but only those whose names are written in the Lamb's book of life."

25. Revelation 22:1 "He showed me a river of the water of life, clear as crystal, coming from the throne of God and of the Lamb."

It is finished.

listen|imagine|view|experience

AUDIO BOOK DOWNLOAD INCLUDED WITH THIS BOOK!

In your hands you hold a complete digital entertainment package. In addition to the paper version, you receive a free download of the audio version of this book. Simply use the code listed below when visiting our website. Once downloaded to your computer, you can listen to the book through your computer's speakers, burn it to an audio CD or save the file to your portable music device (such as Apple's popular iPod) and listen on the go!

How to get your free audio book digital download:

1. Visit www.tatepublishing.com and click on the e|LIVE logo on the home page.
2. Enter the following coupon code:
   d672-a97a-6979-18b7-48cc-ef26-70a0-9135
3. Download the audio book from your e|LIVE digital locker and begin enjoying your new digital entertainment package today!